BIG WORDS for LITTLE KIDS

Advanced Vocabulary for Elementary School Children

Michael Levin M.D.
Charan Langton M.S.

Mountcastle Company
A Reading Lesson Book

BIG WORDS FOR LITTLE KIDS

Michael Levin, M.D.
Charan Langton, M.S.

Edited by Dina Vainer, Ashley Kuhre, and Noel Estabrook
Illustrations by Heather Babcock
Typeset by Pegin S. McDermott

ISBN 0-0913063-13-2
Library of Congress Control Number: 2007938785
Manufactured in the United States of America
Cover Photo from BigStockPhotos

Mountcastle Company
Contact: mntcastle@earthlink.net
www.readinglesson.com

BIG WORDS FOR LITTLE KIDS

Introduction

Not to let a word get in the way of its sentence
Not to let a sentence get in the way of its intention,
But to send your mind out to meet the intention as a guest;
That is understanding.

Chinese proverb, 4th century BC

Building a vocabulary is the most important task children face during their school years. In preschool years, children learn new words by talking to their parents, older siblings, and friends. As they learn to read, their vocabulary grows with every new book. The ability to read, however, does not always translate into the ultimate goals of reading: understanding and reading comprehension.

The current practice in many schools is to expose children to interesting books as a way to improve their vocabulary and reading. Despite steady improvement in reading skills, however, the vocabulary for many children stays virtually still for the first several years of elementary school.

When children encounter unfamiliar words in their reading, they either skip them altogether or try to guess the meaning by the context. Both approaches are inadequate. The new word never enters the active vocabulary, and the next time the child comes across the same word, she would either dismiss it or keep on guessing inaccurate meaning. Incidental learning becomes accidental learning.

The advantages of the *Big Words for Little Kids* program

There are many vocabulary books that use funny stories or selection of new and interesting words in place of a systematic vocabulary approach. When developing the **Big Words for Little Kids** program, we took a proven vocabulary learning approach and adjusted it to the level of a younger child. Our approach is systematic and the store of words we teach though challenging, are suitable for a child at this stage of development. We use only the words that young children are likely to encounter in their everyday reading or while listening to the radio or watching television.

This method of teaching vocabulary, known as the generative program, is more efficient and effective than an unsystematic approach. Children using the **Big Words for Little Kids** program will learn a systematic approach to learning roots and families of words. After becoming comfortable with breaking the familiar words into their parts – prefixes, suffixes, and roots – students will be able to transfer the meaning of these parts to new words.

In the **Big Words for Little Kids** book, your child will learn a variety of methods for attacking unknown words by using his or her knowledge of familiar words. The program teaches the Greek and Latin roots, prefixes, and suffixes of words. Each new root your child learns will enable him or her to learn the meaning of other related words. The combination of generative vocabulary building technique with developmentally appropriate and gradually progressing sets of words makes the **Big Words for Little Kids** program an ideal teaching tool for young readers.

How to teach with the *Big Words for Little Kids* program

Each section of the book has a root, prefix, or suffix accompanied by four to five examples, a tidbit, exercises, and challenging words. There are sample sentences for each new word, one using the big word, the second using a familiar alternative.

A tidbit is a vignette using one of the new words. The two exercises – fill in the blank and multiple choice – do not require writing and can be done verbally.

We also ask that your child make sentences using the "big words." At the end of each section you will find challenge words. Children should look up these words in the dictionary and try to understand the meaning of the word. For very young children, these words might be very challenging indeed and you can skip them.

We suggest you do one section per week.

Roots

Most "big" words in our language came from other languages. There are two languages that gave us most of our scientific and technical words: Greek and Latin. The Greek words came from the language of the ancient Greeks and many old roots can be found in the Modern Greek language. Latin roots and prefixes came from the Ancient Romans. No one uses Latin or the old Greek for everyday speech anymore, but the old languages gave life to several European languages: Italian, Spanish, French, and several others.

The root is the base part of the word, usually in the middle that comes directly from these languages. Often it is has different spellings.

Prefixes

A prefix is a letter or group of letters added at the front of a root or "base word" to change its meaning. According to Dr. H. Thompson Fillmer of the University of Florida in the article, "A Generative Vocabulary Program for Grades 4-6," of the 20,000 most common English words, five thousand have prefixes, and 80% use one of the following prefixes:

ab- (away from)
ad- (to, toward)
com-/con-/co- (with, together)
de- (away, from, downward)

dis- (not, reversal)
en- (in, into, to cover)
ex- (out of, former)
in- (into, not)
pre- (before)
pro- (in favor of, for, before)
re- (again, restore)
sub- (under, beneath)
un- (not, do the opposite of)

Suffixes

A suffix is a letter or group of letters added to the end of a word to change its meaning. Suffixes may also turn a verb into noun or a noun into an adjective. Suffixes do not change the meaning of the words as much as prefixes do. In addition to universal suffixes, such as -s (book, books), -ed (talk, talked), -ing (call, calling), etc., by the beginning of elementary school the children are already familiar with comparative suffixes -er (tall, taller) and -est (cool, coolest). Other common suffixes are:

-ic, ical (dealing with)
-ish (like)
-ist (one who)
-fy (to make)
-ly (manner of)
-ment (result of)
-al (related to)
-ism (belief in)
-less (without)
-let (little)
-logy (science of)
-ness (state of being)
-or (one who)
-ory (where item is made)
-ward (in direction of)

We will introduce and reinforce several of these prefixes and suffixes in the **Big Words for Little Kids** book. It is important to engage your child in interactive games by asking them to either guess the meaning of the words with knowledge of their prefixes and suffixes or create new words. For example, it will be fun for a child to guess the meaning of the words "dispose" and "disgrace" after learning the prefix *dis-* (which means not) or create a new word with the suffix *-less*, like ice cream-less, jacket-less, or videogame-less.

Children can generate new words by adding familiar prefixes and suffixes to new roots. They can further advance their vocabulary through the study of new words and reading. For our course, we have selected a small subset of roots and words with concrete meaning that are easier for young children to understand.

We welcome your suggestions and hope that you will share your experiences with us.

Best wishes,

Michael Levin, MD
Charan Langton, MS
mntcastle@earthlink.net

UN

The prefix **un-** means **not**.

Unable: not having the skill to do something
John liked to sit at the piano even though he <u>was unable</u> to play it.
John liked to sit at the piano even though he <u>could not</u> play it.

Unwelcome: not wanted, not received kindly, not invited
He felt like an <u>unwelcome</u> guest at his cousin's birthday party.
He felt like a <u>not invited</u> guest at his cousin's birthday party.

Uneducated: not schooled, without learning
Anyone who drops out of school will go through life <u>uneducated</u>.
Anyone who drops out of school will go through life <u>not schooled and without learning.</u>

Unhurried: not in a rush
Trevor wanted to appear <u>unhurried</u> as he slowly walked up to the door.
Trevor wanted to appear <u>not in a rush</u> as he slowly walked up to the door.

You may create many new words with the prefix **un-**.

believable	**un**believable
changed	**un**changed
clear	**un**clear
forgettable	**un**forgettable
known	**un**known
mask	**un**mask

Tidbit

In the country of Croatia, a local television station challenged the Guinness World Record for the longest non-stop talk-show. The broadcast lasted 35 hours and will become the longest **uninterrupted** television broadcasting if confirmed by Guinness officials. The previous 33-hour record was held by a television station from New York City.

Fill in each sentence with the correct word:

Unwelcome   Uneducated   Unhurried   Unable

1. Ben remained silent when the class talked about baseball. He knew little about the game and was afraid to appear _____ to others.

2. The young detective felt uneasy and _____ in the company of older police officers.

3. When the register at the store broke, the cashier quit. She said she was _____ to add numbers in her head.

4. When she practiced shooting free throws in basketball, Carrie found it was best to be calm and _____.

Choose the correct definition:

1. **Unwelcome**
   a. not in a rush
   b. not thankful
   c. not wanted
   d. not learned or schooled

2. **Uneducated**
   a. not in a rush
   b. not wanted
   c. not learned
   d. lazy

3. **Unable**
   a. not having the skill
   b. not in a rush
   c. not learned or schooled
   d. not wanted

4. **Unhurried**
   a. not in a rush
   b. not wanted
   c. quickly and sloppily
   d. not learned or schooled

Make a sentence with each of the following words:

Unhurried   Unable   Uneducated   Unwelcome

Challenge Words, look up these words in the dictionary:

Unfamiliar   Unforgiven   Untrained

Nurse: *How much do you weigh, Sarah?*
Sarah: *88 pounds, with my glasses.*
Nurse: *Why with glasses?*
Sarah: *Because without my glasses I am **unable** to see the numbers.*

LESS

The suffix -**less** means **without.**

Fearless: not scared, without fear
The knight was <u>fearless</u> even when facing a dragon.
The knight was <u>not scared</u> even when facing a dragon.

Effortless: easily, without effort
Kangaroo's amazing jumps looked <u>effortless</u>.
Kangaroo's amazing jumps looked <u>easy, without effort</u>.

Hopeless: without hope, not possible
Jenny thought learning big words was <u>hopeless</u> until she tried.
Jenny thought learning big words <u>wasn't possible</u> until she tried.

Tireless: without getting tired, hard working, determined
Sam is <u>tireless</u> when doing math. He works on a problem until he gets it right.
Sam is <u>working hard</u> when he does math. He works on a problem until he gets it right.

Tasteless: in poor taste, bad manners
Alice finds practical jokes to be dumb and <u>tasteless</u>.
Alice finds practical jokes to be dumb and <u>in poor taste</u>.

There are other words with the suffix -**less**:

Pointless: without point, without meaning or reason
Purposeless: without purpose, without goal
Heartless: lacking kindness and feelings, lacking courage
Useless: serving no use

Tidbit

 Jet, the dog, is a great example of being **fearless** in the face of danger. His 10-year-old owner, Kevin Haskell, was hiking with his family and his black lab, Jet, when he heard something in the grass. Jet fearlessly jumped in front of his owner to protect him and got bitten twice in the chest by a rattlesnake! Jet saved his friend's life, and had to go to the doctor. Jet soon went home to his family healthy again. Can you imagine a cat protecting its owner from a rattlesnake?

Fill in each sentence with the correct word:

Fearless   Effortless   Hopeless   Tireless

1. At first Jamie's piano playing looked _____ , but his mom knew that he would be _____ with his daily practices and succeed in the end.

2. Lindsey stood _____ in front of the tall, scary climbing wall; then she went up all the way to the top. She did it so well that from the ground her climb looked _____ .

3. Jack's sister wants to go to medical school and is _____ in her studies.

4. The clown made riding the unicycle look _____ .

Choose the correct definition:

1. **Fearless**
   a. without effort
   b. having no ears
   c. not wearing fur
   d. not scared

2. **Effortless**
   a. not wanting any help
   b. easily, without effort
   c. not afraid
   d. not having a fort

3. **Hopeless**
   a. impossible, without hope
   b. a rattlesnake
   c. not having a home
   d. hard working

4. **Tireless**
   a. a tank
   b. hard working, determined
   c. not having to work hard
   d. not afraid

Make a sentence with each of the following words:

Tireless   Effortless   Fearless   Hopeless

Make four new words with suffix less
Example: without a brain - brainless
          without price - priceless

*To write with a broken pencil is **pointless**!*

IN

The prefix -**in** means **not**. Sometimes this prefix also means **in**.
If the root of the word starts with *m, b,* or *p* the prefix **in** changes to **im**.

Invisible: can't be seen, hidden
The house is <u>invisible</u> from this side of the hill.
The house <u>can't be seen</u> from this side of the hill.

Inarticulate: unable to speak clearly or well, speechless
Jordan memorized his speech because he didn't want to sound <u>inarticulate</u> in front of the whole class.
Jordan memorized his speech because he didn't want to sound like he was <u>unable to speak clearly</u> in front of the whole class.

Incapable: not capable, unable, helpless, inept
Darren is <u>incapable</u> of lying to his friends.
Darren is <u>not able to</u> lie to his friends.

Impossible: not possible, could not happen or be done, unable to control
It is <u>impossible</u> to live in the same house with my <u>impossible</u> pet parrot.
It is <u>not possible</u> to live in the same house with my pet parrot that <u>no one can control</u>.

Improbable: not likely, unlikely to be true, not believable
The story of aliens stealing Lyle's homework was interesting but highly <u>improbable</u>.
The story of aliens stealing Lyle's homework was interesting but highly <u>unlikely</u>.

Immortal: never dying, never to be forgotten, unforgettable
The ancient Greeks built beautiful temples for their <u>immortal</u> gods.
The ancient Greeks built beautiful temples for their <u>undying</u> gods.

Tidbit

Pharaoh means "Great House" and is the Egyptian word for king. Pharaohs believed in **immortality**. They also believed that when a person died they really didn't die. They ordered building of the pyramids in the shape of the first mountain from which the Egyptian believed the earth was created. The Egyptians also believed that the souls of their pharaohs were launched magically through the hole near the tip of the pyramid into the sky, the "**immortal** place."

Fill in each sentence with the correct word:

Invisible   Inarticulate   Incapable   Impossible   Improbable

1. The woman who gave us directions was kind but _____, we couldn't understand a word of her explanation.

2. The chances to win the lottery were not _____, but very _____.

3. H.G. Wells novel "The _____ Man" is a story about a scientist who didn't want to be seen.

4. Byron broke his wrist and was _____ of playing his guitar for a whole month.

Choose the correct definition:

1. **Incapable**
   a. not possible
   b. unlikely
   c. not able
   d. never dying

2. **Impossible**
   a. not possible
   b. unlikely
   c. not able
   d. never dying

3. **Improbable**
   a. not possible
   b. unlikely
   c. not able
   d. never dying

4. **Immortal**
   a. not possible
   b. unlikely
   c. not able
   d. never dying

Challenge Words, look up these words in the dictionary:

Inadequate   Imperfect

Nurse: *Doctor, there is The **Invisible** Man in the waiting room.*
Doctor: *Please tell him that I am unable to see him today.*

ANT and ANTI

Latin prefixes **ant-** and **anti-** mean **against, opposite**, or **opposing**.

Antidote: a medicine used to cure poisonous bites
Carlos was afraid of needles but took the antidote after a spider bit him.
Carlos was afraid of needles but took the medicine that helps fight the poison after a spider bit him.

Antipathy: to dislike or be hostile toward someone
The girls worked together on the project in spite of their antipathy toward one another.
The girls worked together on the project in spite of their dislike toward one another.

Antagonist: an enemy or opponent, often in a book or story
Lex Luthor was Superman's long-time antagonist.
Lex Luthor was Superman's long-time enemy.

Antonym: a word that means the opposite of another word
Everyone knows hot is the antonym of cold, but what's the antonym of warm?
Everyone knows hot is the opposite of cold, but what word is the opposite of warm?

Confusion Alerts!

1. Do not confuse **anti-** with **ante-**, which means **before**. We will be learning about prefix **ante-** in the next lesson.

2. Don't confuse the prefix **ant-** with the insects of the same name, anteater does not mean against eaters.

Tidbit

 Since it was 1965 before the first **antiperspirant** (perspire means to sweat) was invented, people for centuries used deodorants - heavy colognes and perfumes to cover up body odor caused by sweating. Men and women who didn't wash for months covered themselves in flowery scents - which must have smelled pretty gross! Washerwomen would set clothes out to dry on lavender bushes to help make them smell better but that couldn't have helped much. Then came the invention of **antiperspirant** from aluminum. Now we can run miles and still smell fresh and sweet. Nah!

Fill in each sentence with the correct word:

Antonym   Antagonists   Antipathy   Antidote

1. Joel had always felt a little _____ toward Mike since the time when Mike spilled his entire lunch in Joel's lap.

2. There wouldn't be many good stories if the heroes never faced _____.

3. When the teacher asked the class what they thought the _____ of sad was, Bridget screamed "summer vacation!"

4. Michael creatively called the weekly soccer games with his best friends an _____ to boredom.

Choose the correct definition:

1. **Antonym**
   a. hostility or dislike
   b. something unimportant
   c. a person who doesn't like others
   d. opposite meaning to another word

2. **Antagonist**
   a. the opposite of agony
   b. a bad organ player
   c. dislike and hostility
   d. an enemy

3. **Antipathy**
   a. dislike or hostility
   b. disrespectful and rude behavior
   c. a medication that fights poison
   d. opposite meaning to another word

4. **Antidote**
   a. a medication that fights poison
   b. the opposite of a dot, like a circle
   c. opposite meaning to another word
   d. dislike and hatred

Make a sentence with each of the following words:

Antonym   Antagonist   Antipathy   Antidote

Challenge Words, look up these words in the dictionary:

Antifreeze   Antihero   Antarctic

The boy is praying: *Please, please move Canada to* **Antarctica**.
Mom: *Why Antarctica?*
Boy: *Because that's what I wrote in my test.*

ANTE and POST

The Latin prefix **ante-** means **before**.
The Latin prefix **post-** means **after**.

Anteroom: a room that comes before another room
Mrs. Fancy dropped her coat in the <u>anteroom</u> and stormed into the office.
Mrs. Fancy dropped her coat in the <u>room before</u> and stormed into the office.

Anterior: placed before or in front of
His big nose was <u>anterior</u> to his face.
His big nose was <u>in front</u> of his face.

Antebellum (the word bellum means war): a time period before a war, specifically the American Civil War
Gone with the Wind is a book that describes <u>antebellum</u> life.
Gone with the Wind is a book that describes life <u>before the American Civil War</u>.

Posterior: placed behind or in the back
The bear stood on its <u>posterior</u> legs and roared.
The bear stood on its <u>back</u> legs and roared.

Postnatal: after the birth
Gail gave the puppies a <u>postnatal</u> checkup and put them next to the mother.
Gail gave the puppies an <u>after birth</u> checkup and put them next to the mother.

Postpone: put off until later, delay
Little Red Riding Hood had to <u>postpone</u> her planned visit to her grandmother.
Little Red Riding Hood had to <u>delay</u> her planned visit to her grandmother.

Tidbit

You have undoubtedly seen the initials A.M. and P.M. on your clock or on paper. Do you know what they mean? A.M. stands for **Ante Meridiem** and means before noon. P.M. stands for **Post Meridiem** and means after noon. We use these abbreviations when we want to tell what part of the day we mean. The 12-hour clock was invented in ancient Egypt and then rediscovered by the Romans. Most modern clocks and watches use the 12 hour system. In the military and in many countries all over the world, people use the 24 hour system to measure time and have no need to tell A.M. from P.M.

Fill in each sentence with the correct word:

Anteroom   Anterior   Postpone   Postnatal   Antebellum

1. A historian who examined the pocket watch was sure it was an
   _____ piece dating from about five years before the War.

2. After carefully opening the front door, a burglar found himself in a large
   _____ filled with members of a local boxing club.

3. Juan tried to convince the teacher to _____ the final exam for two
   weeks, but she did not change her mind.

4. The bodybuilder spent more time building his _____ muscles and
   less time on his posterior.

Choose the correct definition:

1. **Anterior**
   a. placed in front   c. placed above
   b. placed behind   d. happened later

2. **Antebellum**
   a. very early   c. a sundial
   b. very late   d. before the War

3. **Postpone**
   a. to do it early   c. to put it off
   b. after a birth   d. after dinner

4. **Postnatal**
   a. after a birth   c. after a war
   b. after dinner   d. afternoon

Make a sentence with each of the following words:

Anterior   Postpone   Posterior   Postnatal

Challenge Words, look up these words in the dictionary:

Antecedent   Postprandial   Postmortem

The teacher: *Why do we see lightning before we hear thunder.*
Student: *Because the eyes are **anterior** and the ears are **posterior**.*

HYPO and HYPER

The Greek prefix **hypo-** means **low, under**, or **less**.
The Greek prefix **hyper-** means **over, above** or **too much**.
You can use the same roots or words with either prefix.

Hypoactive: slow, under-active
Hyperactive: fast moving, highly active, always on the go
My two hamsters are so different, Snooze is hypoactive but Cruise is hyperactive.
My two hamsters are so different, Snooze moves slowly but Cruise moves very fast.

Hyposensitive: less sensitive than others about feelings
Hypersensitive: excessively sensitive, touchy, easy to get upset
Everyone thought Mr. Stone was rude because he was hyposensitive. This was bad for his wife Kathy, who was hypersensitive and would cry at anything he said.
Everyone thought Mr. Stone was rude because he did not care about others' feelings. This was bad for his wife Kathy who was very sensitive and easy to get upset and would cry at anything he said.

Hypotension: a condition of low blood pressure
Hypertension: a condition of high blood pressure
Quite the opposite of having hypotension, Mr. Donny's doctor thought he would have dangerous hypertension by the time he was 50 years old.
Quite the opposite of having low blood pressure, Mr. Donny's doctor thought he would have dangerous high blood pressure by the time he was 50 years old.

Other words with the prefix **hypo**:
Hypothermia (therm means temperature) - a condition with low temperature
Hyperthermia - a condition with high temperature
Hypodermic (derm means skin) - thin short needle that goes just under the skin but not much deeper. The injections are given with hypodermic needles.

Other words with the prefix **hyper**:
Hypercritical - very critical, finding faults in everyone and everything
Hyperhydrosis - a disorder with a lot of sweating, all over or in one place

Tidbit

Any speed that is faster than the speed of sound is called **supersonic**. The speed of sound is 761 miles per hour, which is more than ten times faster than the highest speed allowed on American highways. The American pilot Chuck Yeager was the first pilot to break sound speed barrier in an airplane in 1947. The term **hypersonic** is used to describe the airplanes moving at a speed way above supersonic.

You can guess the meaning of the words with prefix **hyper**:
Hyper-thirsty means …
Hyper-smart means …
Hyper-fast means …
Hyper-hungry means …
Hyper-late means …

You can also make your own words with prefix **hyper**:
Very tired will be hyper-tired
Very stupid will be …
Very nice will be …
Very honest will be …

Choose the correct definition:

1. **Hypertension**
   a. fast moving
   b. high blood pressure
   c. a nervous feeling before a test
   d. focusing well, paying attention

2. **Hypersonic**
   a. really loud
   b. very quiet
   c. slow moving
   d. faster than the speed of sound

3. **Hypotension**
   a. stress-free
   b. full of stress
   c. high blood pressure
   d. low blood pressure

4. **Hyperactive**
   a. high blood pressure
   b. having a full-time acting job
   c. moving too fast, always on the go
   d. fresh water fish

First Mom: *These two boys in the photograph, are they your twins?*
Second Mom: *No, I have only one child but he is very **hyperactive**.*

CO, CON, and COM

These prefixes mean **with** or **together.**

Cooperate: to work together, getting along together
The teacher asked everyone to <u>cooperate</u> to make a skit for the talent show.
The teacher asked everyone to <u>work together</u> to make a skit for the talent show.

Confidence: sharing trust, belief in self, belief in other person to keep a secret
June is not sure she has enough <u>confidence</u> to dance in front of the whole school.
June is not sure she has enough <u>belief in herself</u> to dance in front of the whole school.

Conspire: to act or plan together secretly
The boys <u>conspired</u> to run away at night but fell asleep and ruined their plan.
The boys <u>secretly planned</u> to run away at night but fell asleep and ruined their plan.

Component: a part of a whole, a piece that goes together with other pieces to make a whole
Ali saw that some <u>components</u> from his watch were left over after he put it back together.
Ali saw that some <u>parts</u> from his watch were left over after he put it back together.

Compassion: to share in another's feelings, understanding and caring
Leo showed <u>compassion</u> by reading a book to his blind neighbor.
Leo showed <u>understanding and caring</u> by reading a book to his blind neighbor.

Tidbit

 Today, we don't think twice about men and women going to the same college. But, up until the 19th century, nobody thought that educating girls was necessary - and nobody let them into college! Even though most school teachers were women, colleges still didn't allow women to study there, so many teachers were barely better educated than their students! Oberlin College in Ohio was one of the first college to become a **coeducational**, or coed, school in 1837. This was only the first time in American history that men and women studied together.

Fill in each sentence with the correct word:

Confidence   Cooperate   Component   Compassion   Conspired

1. Their mom told them that if they couldn't learn to _____ and stop arguing, she wasn't taking them to the park. She said that getting along is a necessary _____ of happy family life.

2. Nothing the teacher did helped to give Arnold the _____ he needed to sing.

3. At the end of the day, tired of trying, the teacher let Arnold go home out of pure _____.

4. When the next day everyone refused to sing, the teacher suspect that the whole choir _____ against him.

Choose the correct definition:

1. **Conspire**
   a. to work together   c. to plot together
   b. to join together   d. to talk together

2. **Confidence**
   a. to plot together   c. believing in self
   b. to work together   d. to have all parts together

3. **Cooperate**
   a. to mix or put together   c. to work together
   b. to talk together   d. to trust each other

4. **Compassion**
   a. to respect   c. to join together
   b. to feel for someone   d. to like someone

Make a sentence with each of the following words:

Confidence   Cooperate   Component   Compassion   Conspire

Challenge Words, look up these words in the dictionary:

Commotion   Concentrate

Why are you staring at this can of frozen orange juice?
It says **concentrate**!

GEN

The root **gen-** means **birth, growth,** or **beginning**.

General: relating to all kinds, common; also, a military rank
The <u>general</u> opinion is that you develop a large vocabulary by reading.
The <u>common</u> opinion is that you develop a large vocabulary by reading.

Generous: large; giving and charitable
Sean's Boy Scout troupe got a <u>generous</u> donation from Sean's <u>generous</u> grandpa.
Sean's Boy Scout troupe got a <u>large</u> donation from Sean's <u>giving</u> grandpa.

Genealogy: family tree, a study of family history
Tom learned that he was related to Thomas Jefferson by studying his <u>genealogy</u>.
Tom learned that he was related to Thomas Jefferson by studying his <u>family tree</u>.

Generate: to produce, create, cause to be
Roof-top solar panels can <u>generate</u> enough energy for the whole house.
Roof-top solar panels can <u>produce</u> enough energy for the whole house.

Congenital: a condition from birth or caused by birth
The puppy was deaf, a <u>congenital</u> defect common in Dalmatians.
The puppy was deaf, a <u>condition</u> <u>at birth</u> common in Dalmatians.

Confusion Alert!

The words **congenital** and **congenial** look and sound very similar but have different meanings. **Congenial** means to be **friendly** or **agreeable**. Of course, for some people, being congenial might be congenital.

Tidbit

The word **genius** comes from the root gen. There have been many geniuses over the course of history, and one of them was Leonardo Da Vinci. He is famous for his amazing inventions, sculptures, and paintings. One of his lesser-known inventions was a robot! He drew plans for this human-looking machine more than 500 years ago, around 1495. Though many of his plans are lost, scientists now think that the robot would have been able to open its mouth, sit up, and wave its arms. The design was found in one of Leonardo's sketchbooks. It is not known whether or not he tried to build the device.

Fill in each sentence with the correct word:

General   Generous   Genealogy   Generate   Congenital

1. By tracing her _____ Amber found out that her family had originally come from Turkey.

2. The _____ feeling in the room was happy and excited, as everyone counted down to New Year.

3. The limp in his walk is because of a _____ problem with his leg.

4. Luann's idea seemed to _____ so much enthusiasm, that by the end of the day, dozens of students gathered in front of the school.

5. Michael put a _____ amount of meat loaf on his plate.

Choose the correct definition:

1. **General**
   a. giving
   b. common
   c. a family tree
   d. specific

2. **Generous**
   a. giving, charitable
   b. specific
   c. a military rank
   d. common

3. **Genealogy**
   a. local
   b. the study of genes
   c. a family tree
   d. an oak tree

4. **Congenital**
   a. specific
   b. friendly agreeable
   c. wearing jeans
   d. present at birth

Make a sentence with each of the following words:

General   Generous   Congenital

Challenge Words, look up these words in the dictionary:

Genial   Generator   Generalize

Boy: *When I grow up I want to be a **general**.*
Mom: *But the enemy can shoot you during the war.*
Boy: *Then, can I be the enemy?*

LOG and LOGO

The Greek roots **log-** and **logo-** mean **word, talk,** or **study**.

Logic: good reason, smart thinking, common sense
Karen used <u>logic</u> to figure out who could have stolen her chocolate bar.
Karen used <u>smart thinking</u> to figure out who could have stolen her chocolate bar.

Logical: rational, reasonable, using common-sense
Since Jim's face was smeared with chocolate, it was <u>logical</u> to assume he did it.
Since Jim's face was smeared with chocolate, it was <u>reasonable</u> to assume he did it.

Prologue: an introduction to a play or a book
The play's <u>prologue</u> was almost as long as the play itself.
The play's <u>introduction</u> was almost as long as the play itself.

Epilogue: a closing section of a play or book that adds information
From the <u>epilogue</u> Luke learned that the prince and princess did not live happily ever after.
From the <u>closing section</u> Luke learned that the prince and princess did not live happily ever after.

Logo: a name or symbol that makes a company or product easy to remember
Anybody who sees the swoosh <u>logo</u> quickly recognizes it as Nike.
Anybody who sees the swoosh <u>design</u> quickly recognizes it as Nike.

The suffix **-logy** means science or study. You already know some words with this root. Here are some more:
Geology (*geo* means earth): science or study of the earth
Zoology: science or study of animals
Anthropology (*anthrop* means human): science or study of humans
Criminology: science or study of crime and criminals

Tidbit

 If you've ever gotten food poisoning, you probably know what diarrhea is - yuck! But do you want what **logorrhea** is? People with **logorrhea**, which means "a flow of words," often talk or write so much and so confusingly that other people can't even understand them! In 1996, physicist Alan Sokal sent an article written in the form of **logorrhea** to a scientific journal as a practical joke. Although the article made no sense, it was still published! The magazine editors didn't understand the article but thought it must be about something important.

Fill in each sentence with the correct word:

Logic   Logical   Prologue   Logo

1. Tom was working on his new novel's _____ when the phone rang.

2. Marla thought it was funny that, even though she was in Japan, she could recognize the golden arches of the McDonald's _____.

3. Jimmy used _____ to prove that Bill could not have been the burglar because Jack's wife said that he painting their house at noon.

4. Because Tammy was both smart and clumsy, she knew it wasn't _____ to run away and join the circus.

Choose the correct definition:

1. **Logic**
   a. planning and doing a task
   b. the science of reason
   c. a design or symbol
   d. not being able to stop talking

2. **Epilogue**
   a. the introduction to a book
   b. the science of logic
   c. the end section of a book
   d. reasonable

3. **Logical**
   a. rational, reasonable
   b. a science
   c. doing a task
   d. a symbol used by a company

4. **Logo**
   a. the science of reason
   b. planning and doing a task
   c. something rational
   d. a symbol used by a company

Make a sentence with each of the following words:

Logical   Prologue   Epilogue   Logo

Challenge Words, look up these words in the dictionary:

Monologue (hint: mono means one)
Dialogue (hint: dia means two)

> **Dad:** *Johnny, why do you have F's in all subjects except* **biology***?*
> **Johnny:** *We didn't have a test in* **biology***.*

PRE

The Latin prefix **pre-** means **before**.

Prevent: to avoid or stop something before it happens
Please drive slowly near schools to <u>prevent</u> accidents.
Please drive slowly near schools to <u>avoid</u> accidents.

Prevail: to win over, to succeed
In the final game, our soccer team <u>prevailed</u> and we became the champions.
In the final game, our soccer team <u>won over</u> and we became the champions.

Precocious: intelligent and mature at a young age, ahead of the rest
Andrea was a <u>precocious</u> baby who took her first step at eight months.
Andrea was a <u>more mature than usual</u> baby who took her first step at eight months.

Confusion Alert!
The word **precocious** can be easily confused with the word **precautious**, which means careful.

Precede: to come first, go before
George Washington <u>preceded</u> Abraham Lincoln as President of the United States.
George Washington <u>was</u> the President of the United States <u>before</u> Abraham Lincoln.

Confusion Alert!
The word **precede** might be confused with **proceed**, which means to move along or go ahead.

Tidbit

Many baby animals seem amazingly **precocious** right after they're born. Human babies must be taken care of for years and years before they can survive on their own, while many baby animals, like calves and colts, manage to stand up and run soon after they're born! Another amazing animal is the baby kangaroo, also called a joey. When these tiny joeys are born, they're totally blind and weigh less than 2 grams! But instead of just sitting in their mom's fur after they're born, they climb up their mom's belly and into her pouch! They can't see, and can barely move, but they know where to go and what to do! Now that's **precocious**!

Fill in each sentence with the correct word:

Precocious   Prevent   Prevail   Precede

1. Alex was precautious and always wore his seat belt to _____ getting hurt in a car accident.

2. Tiffany was very _____ . By the time she was eight, she could cook a full dinner by herself.

3. One should _____ any construction with careful planning, even if they're just building a doghouse.

4. Try hard and you will_____ at the end.

You can often guess the meaning of the word by knowing the prefix **pre** and the rest of the word:
Prepay would mean pay before, ahead of time.
Prerecord means to record in advance, before the show or concert actually starts.
And many of you went to **preschool**.

Choose the correct definition:

1. **Prevent**
   a. smart and mature
   b. to avoid before it happens
   c. to get ready
   d. to organize

2. **Prevail**
   a. to avoid before it happens
   b. to get ready
   c. to succeed
   d. smart at a young age

3. **Precocious**
   a. a safety measure
   b. mature at a young age
   c. to avoid something
   d. very careful

Challenge Words, look up these words in the dictionary:

Premonition   Preliminary

In a restaurant a customer calls the waiter.
Waiter: *Do you have any questions about the menu?*
Customer: *How do you **prepare** your chicken?*
Waiter: *We tell them straight: "We will make a sandwich out of you." It's better this way.*

RE

The prefix **re-** means **again.**

Renew: to make new again, to start something again
Ally felt <u>renewed</u> after a long nap and a hot shower.
Ally felt <u>like a new person</u> after a long nap and a hot shower.

Reconsider: to consider or think again, to change an earlier decision
Watching ballet made Jen <u>reconsider</u> her plan to take dance lessons.
Watching ballet made Jen <u>think again</u> about her plan to take dance lessons.

Reimburse: to get money back
Robbie's mom paid for her own ticket on a business trip. Her company said they would <u>reimburse</u> her.
Robbie's mom paid for her own ticket on a business trip. Her company said they would <u>pay her back</u>.

Replica: an imitation, a copy, usually of a work of art
Suresh made a small <u>replica</u> of the Statue of Liberty and brought it to class.
Suresh made a small <u>copy</u> of the Statue of Liberty and brought it to class.

Reiterate: repeat, to say or do again
The professor <u>reiterated</u> the story because it was going to be on the test.
The professor <u>repeated</u> the story because it was going to be on the test.

Many new words can be made by attaching prefix **re-**:

build	**re**build (build again)	name	**re**name
count	**re**count	play	**re**play
create	**re**create	test	**re**test

Tidbit

 Most people try to **recycle** some things. But some people, like Cate and Wayne of New Mexico, are extreme **recyclers**. Over 250 used tires that have been packed with earth and concrete create the basic structure of their house! Wayne and Cate used old wood for the roof, salvaged glass for the windows, and about 13,000 empty soda cans throughout the house. Their three-bedroom home is heated by solar power, and they use a wood-burning stove for cold days. Now that's **recycling**!

Fill in each sentence with the correct word:

Reimbursed   Reiterate   Replica   Renewed   Reconsider

1. Grandma likes to _____ everything she says since she can't hear well and thinks no one else does, either.

2. Andrew had to _____ his feelings about broccoli after he learned that the dip he'd been gobbling up was made out of it.

3. After resting a while, Ali came back to the climbing party with _____ enthusiasm.

4. Linn didn't expect to get _____ for the lunch she bought for her roommate Jenna; she knew Jenna didn't have much money.

5. Linda bought a portrait of the Mona Lisa for five dollars and was shocked to learn that it was only a _____.

Choose the correct definition:

1. **Reconsider**
   a. a military operation
   b. to make new again
   c. to put back in place
   d. to think over

2. **Renewed**
   a. to pay back
   b. to make new again
   c. to think over
   d. to put in place

3. **Replica**
   a. talking back
   b. a political party
   c. a pay back
   d. a copy

4. **Reimburse**
   a. to pay back
   b. to kiss your money goodbye
   c. to think over
   d. to repeat it again

Challenge Words, look up these words in the dictionary:

Rehabilitate   Reform

Did you hear about the scarecrow Mr. Foster put on his farm?
No, why?
*It is so scary that the birds **returned** all of last year's crop.*

SE

This Latin prefix means **without** or **apart**.

Separate: to take apart, to sort, to remove
Justin forgot to <u>separate</u> the whites from the colors when he did the laundry and ended up dyeing all his clothes pink.
Justin forgot to <u>sort</u> the whites from the colors when he did the laundry and ended up dyeing all his clothes pink.

Secretive: not sharing thoughts, cautious, hiding thoughts
Angela was a <u>secretive</u> girl, she never talked about her family.
Angela was a <u>cautious</u> girl, she never talked about her family.

Secluded: set apart, isolated, out of the way
Whenever Jack was upset, he'd go to a <u>secluded</u> place in the woods to be by himself.
Whenever Jack was upset, he'd go to an <u>out of the way</u> place in the woods to be by himself.

Selective: choosing carefully between options, able to tell things apart, choosy
Lisa was so <u>selective</u> that she never wore clothes without a famous brand name.
Lisa was so <u>choosy</u> that she never wore clothes without a famous brand name.

Sever: to separate, divide; to cut or break off
After the big argument, Don decided to <u>sever</u> his realtionship with his friend.
After the big argument, Don decided to <u>cut off</u> his realtionship with his friend.

Confusion Alert!
Don't confuse the verb **sever** with the adjective **severe,** which means harsh, serious, grave, or intense.

Tidbit

Most of us can't swim in icy water for hours or hold our breath for longer than a couple of minutes, but a **select** few have the talent and courage to do things that would kill a normal person. Tanya Streeter's amazing lungs and willpower have allowed her to swim 525 feet, the length of a 50-story building, on just one breath. Doctors have figured out that Tanya's lungs can take in almost twice the amount of oxygen as most women her size!

Fill in each sentence with the correct word:

Selective   Secluded   Secretive   Separate

1. Sarah wasn't _____ for very long; by the end of the day we knew everything about her.

2. Our dog went to a _____ part of the garage to have her puppies.

3. The varsity team was so _____ about whom they picked that Nick was worried about his chances.

4. Josh had a weird way of eating salad: he'd _____ all the vegetables and put them in little piles before he ate them.

Choose the correct definition:

1. **Separate**
   a. hidden
   b. choosy, picky
   c. to take apart, to sort
   d. an isolated spot

2. **Secretive**
   a. not sharing thoughts
   b. telling lies
   c. choosing carefully
   d. remote

3. **Secluded**
   a. choosy
   b. holding your breath
   c. set apart, isolated, out of the way
   d. the remote control

4. **Selective**
   a. isolated
   b. to keep concealed
   c. to take apart
   d. choosing carefully between things

Make a sentence with each of the following words:

Selective   Secluded   Secretive   Separate

Challenge Words, look up these words in the dictionary:

Sequester   Segregate

Baby's secret: *If at first you don't succeed, cry, cry again.*

GRAPH

The Greek root **graph** means to **write**.

Graph: A written diagram or chart
For her science project, Deb drew a <u>graph</u> of how tall her pea plants grew in four weeks.
For her science project, Deb drew a <u>chart</u> of how tall her pea plants grew in four weeks.

Calligraphy (*calli* means beautiful): beautiful and fancy handwriting
The invitation to Alicia's graduation was written in <u>calligraphy.</u>
The invitation to Alicia's graduation was written in <u>beautiful handwriting</u>.

Photograph: a picture taken with a camera
Sara took a silly <u>photograph</u> of George in a gorilla suit.
Sara took a silly <u>picture</u> of George in a gorilla suit.

Geography: study of the people and places on Earth
Kim was a good <u>geography</u> student who knew the capitals of all the African nations.
Kim was a good student of the <u>places on Earth</u> who knew the capitals of all the African nations.

Orthography (*ortho* means straight): spelling rules; spelling as a school subject
Kyle's writing was known for perfect <u>orthography</u>.
Kyle's writing was known for perfect <u>spelling</u>.

Tidbit

A **polygraph** is a lie-detector machine. It works by measuring changes in heartbeat, blood pressure, and breathing of a person during an interview. The idea of the **polygraph** is that when you lie about something, you get nervous, and when you get nervous your heart beats faster, you start breathing harder, and you sweat. A **polygraph's** lines can show tiny changes in someone's body when someone may be telling a lie. Police uses the **polygraph** machine to check if a suspect is telling the truth.

Fill in each sentence with the correct word:

Graph   Calligraphy   Photograph   Geography

1. Jan bought a set of pens and ink to learn the art of _____ .

2. The _____ of the land was diverse: there were mountains and valleys, rivers and oceans.

3. Annie's sister always tried to _____ her when she was doing silly things, like eating with her mouth open or picking her nose.

4. The teacher made a _____ comparing the heights of everyone in class.

Choose the correct definition:

1. **Graph**
   a. the stuff inside a pencil
   b. a chart or diagram
   c. a lie-detector
   d. a study of the world

2. **Calligraphy**
   a. a picture
   b. writing about California
   c. beautiful writing
   d. calling to write a story

3. **Photograph**
   a. a lie-detector
   b. study of the world
   c. a plant
   d. a picture from a camera

4. **Geography**
   a. the study of the Earth
   b. a car model
   c. a picture
   d. a chart or diagram

Make a sentence with each of the following words:

Graph   Calligraphy   Photograph   Geography

Challenge Words, look up these words in the dictionary:

Choreography (hint: *choreo* means dance)
Telegraph (hint: *tele* means distance, far)

Brother: *In my **geography** class, I couldn't find Alaska.*
Little sister: *What a loser! You probably dropped it somewhere.*

SCRIB and SCRIPT

The Latin roots **scrib** and **script** mean **writing.**

Subscribe (sub means under): to sign one's name at the end of a document, under the text; an agreement to pay for receiving magazines or newspapers in the mail
I saved all my allowance to <u>subscribe</u> to Skateboarding Monthly magazine.
I saved all my allowance to <u>receive in the mail</u> Skateboarding Monthly magazine.

Prescribe: to order a medicine, set the rules
For my sore throat the doctor <u>prescribed</u> the bitterest medicine in the world.
For my sore throat the doctor <u>ordered</u> the bitterest medicine in the world.

Confusion alert!

Prescribe and **proscribe** share the same root but their prefixes give the words different meanings. **Proscribe** means to exclude, prohibit, or forbid.

Script: style of handwriting, an original document, and also the text of a play or movie
When Sergio read the <u>script</u> of his new comedy everyone laughed.
When Sergio read the <u>text</u> of his new comedy everyone laughed.

Transcript: a complete copy of a document, for example student's grades
Valery was so proud of her <u>transcript</u> that she framed it and put it on the wall.
Valery was so proud of her <u>grades</u> that she framed them and put them on the wall.

Postscript: an additional message at the end of a letter, usually written as PS or P.S.
At the end of the letter she wrote: **P.S.** Uncle Bill sends his love.

Tidbit

 Conscription is the law in some countries for their citizens, mostly men, to serve in the armed forces. Conscription, also known as a draft, existed since colonial times and had been used for various wars. It ended in 1973. Many countries, among them the United States, do not demand that all men serve in the military but rely on volunteers and professional servicemen.

Fill in each sentence with the correct word:

Subscribe   Prescribed   Script   Transcripts   Postscript

1. Arthur hid his school _____ and hoped the parents never ask for them.

2. Dr. Malik suggested that I _____ to a science magazine.

3. Colin got sick and the doctor _____ cough syrup.

4. My grandmother always wrote her letters by hand, using neat _____ with a _____ at the end with best wishes to the family.

Choose the correct definition:

1. **Subscribe**
   a. write a play
   b. order a medicine
   c. to order a magazine
   d. to forbid

2. **Prescribe**
   a. write a play
   b. order a medicine
   c. to sign under a document
   d. to forbid

3. **Transcript**
   a. a text for a play
   b. school grades
   c. a signed document
   d. at the end of a letter

4. **Postscript**
   a. a text for a play
   b. school grades
   c. a signed document
   d. at the end of a letter

Make a sentence with each of the following words:

Subscribe   Prescribe   Script   Transcripts

Challenge Words, look up these words in the dictionary:

Inscription   Describe   Circumscribe

Patient: *Doctor, every night I dream of rats playing baseball.*
Doctor: *I'll **prescribe** you a medicine. Take it tonight and sleep well.*
Patient: *Can I start Monday? This weekend they have playoffs.*

PHOTO

The Greek root **photo** means **light**.

Photophobia (*phobia* means fear): fear or sensitivity to light
Severe headaches might cause <u>photophobia</u>.
Severe headaches might cause <u>sensitivity to light</u>.

Photogenic: looking good in photographs
Margaret was so <u>photogenic</u>, she looked better in her pictures than she did in person.
Margaret <u>looked good in her photos</u>, even better than she did in person.

Photometer: a device that measures the strength of light
Professional photographers use a <u>photometer</u> to adjust the setting of the camera.
Professional photographers use a <u>light-measuring device</u> to adjust the setting of the camera.

Photosynthesis: the process by which plants take light and produce sugars for energy
Jodie put her flowerpot in the closet not knowing that plants needed <u>photosynthesis</u> to grow.
Jodie put her flowerpot in the closet not knowing that plants needed <u>sugars produced by light</u> to grow.

Tidbit

The word **photography** is a combination of the Greek roots *photo*, meaning *light*, and *graph*, meaning to *write*. Light is the most important part of **photography** because of the way certain **photosensitive** chemicals change when light is shone upon them. Sir John F.W. Herschel first used the word **photography** in 1839 to describe a way of recording images by the contact of light on a sensitive material. In 1827, the inventor of **photography**, Joseph Nicéphore Niépce, took eight whole hours to make the very first **photograph**. It would be another dozen years before anyone could take a picture in less than 30 minutes and keep it from disappearing.

Fill in each sentence with the correct word:

Photophobia   Photogenic   Photometer   Photosynthesis

1. The yearbook picture of the usually _____ Christine was terrible because the picture was taken while she was sneezing.

2. The picture came out dark and blurry because the photographer forgot to use the _____.

3. For his science project, Jay studied what kind of light for plants is the best for _____.

Choose the correct definition:

1. **Photophobia**
   - a. a writing instrument
   - b. a picture taken from a camera
   - c. sensitivity to light
   - d. a process that plants use

2. **Photogenic**
   - a. plants use it for energy
   - b. a picture of genes
   - c. a tool used to measure light
   - d. looking good in photographs

3. **Photometer**
   - a. a person who takes photographs
   - b. a picture taken from a camera
   - c. looking good in photos
   - d. the device a photographer might use

4. **Photosynthesis**
   - a. a person who takes photos
   - b. the way plant turns light into sugar
   - c. looking good in photos
   - d. a picture taken from a camera

Make a sentence with each of the following words:

Photometer   Photogenic   Photosynthesis

Challenge Words, look up these words in the dictionary:

Photocopy   Photosensitive

*A father in the newborn nursery is taking a **photograph** after **photograph** of his newborn baby girl.*
The nurse: *You took so many pictures. Is this your first child?*
Dad: *This is my third baby but it's my first camera.*

INTER

The prefix **inter-** means **between** or **among**.

Interfere: to disrupt, to meddle
It is not polite to interfere in other people's business.
It is not polite to meddle in other people's business.

Intervene: to come or appear between two things to make a change
The boys were already arguing for an hour when the coach decided to intervene.
The boys were already arguing for an hour when the coach decided to come between.

Intercept: to stop something between the time it's sent and received
James was able to intercept the letter before Sally could read it.
James was able to stop the letter before Sally could read it.

Interdependent: to be dependent on each other
Wolves run in packs because they are interdependent and can't survive alone.
Wolves run in packs because they depend on each other and can't survive alone.

Interlude: an in-between period, break
There was a brief interlude between Acts I and II of the play.
There was a brief break between Acts I and II of the play.

Interstate: between states
Interstate trade between Texas and Florida increased last year.
Trade between Texas and Florida increased last year.

Confusion Alert!

The words **interstate** and **intrastate** look and sound very similar but have different, opposing meaning. Interstate (inter, meaning between) means between the states, while intrastate (intra, being inside) means within the state.

Tidbit

The first superhighway to open in the United States was the Pennsylvania Turnpike in 1940. This launched a movement to create the American superhighway network connecting all of the states, commonly known as the **Interstate** Highway System. Authorized in 1944 by an act of Congress, construction took thirty years to complete. The American **Interstate** Highway System encompasses over 42,000 miles of roads, many of them superhighways that connect all 48 continental states.

Big Words for Little Kids

Fill in each sentence with the correct word:

Interstate   Interlude   Intercept   Interfere

1. They decided to leave the small rural road and get on the big _____ highway that connects California and Nevada.

2. After the quarterback threw the pass, the defender was able to _____ it before it reached the receiver.

3. During the _____, Donovan sneaked behind the curtains and shook the conductor's hand.

4. It was difficult for Samantha not to _____ when her friends were arguing right in front of her.

Choose the correct definition:

1. **Interlude**
   a. a period between
   b. between states
   c. to meddle
   d. dependent upon each other

2. **Intercept**
   a. a period between
   b. a period between May and June
   c. between states
   d. take between the sending and delivery

3. **Interstate**
   a. a period between
   b. between states
   c. within one state
   d. time between the sending and delivery

4. **Interfere**
   a. a feeling in between afraid & scared
   b. between states
   c. to meddle
   d. a period between two holidays

Make a sentence with each of the following words:

Interstate   Interfere   Intercept

Challenge Words, look up these words in the dictionary:

Interaction   Interject

> **Teacher:** *Julie, please give me a sentence starting with "I."*
> **Julie:** *I is...*
> **Teacher interrupts:** *No, Julie. Always say, "I am."*
> **Julie:** *All right . . . "I am the ninth letter of the alphabet."*

BIO, VIV and VITA

The Greek root **bio** means **life**.
The Latin roots **viv** and **vita** also mean life.

Biology: the study of living things
James was interested in <u>biology</u> because he wanted to be a doctor.
James was interested in <u>studying living things</u> because he wanted to be a doctor.

Biography: a life story
After reading the actor's <u>biography</u>, Stephanie rented all of his movies.
After reading the actor's <u>life story</u>, Stephanie rented all of his movies.

Antibiotic: a medicine that kills germs
Although the <u>antibiotic</u> tasted terrible, Joey had to drink it every day to get better.
Although the <u>medicine that kills germs</u> tasted terrible, Joey had to drink it every day to get better.

Vivid: full of life, lively; brightly colored; colorful, lifelike images in mind
Lately, Monica had a lot of <u>vivid</u> dreams.
Lately, Monica had a lot of <u>colorful, lifelike</u> dreams.

Vital: necessary, important for life
It is <u>vital</u> that everyone attends the lecture on healthy eating habits.
It is <u>necessary</u> that everyone attends the lecture on healthy eating habits.

Tidbit

Bioluminescence (the word lumen means light) is light produced by living things using bacteria or chemicals stored in their bodies. Many creatures, like fireflies and jellyfish, produce light. Other cool organisms that light up just by living are squid and some deep sea fish that have their own "night light" hanging in front of their heads. In some places you can find millions and millions of tiny single-celled **bioluminescent** creatures that make the sea sparkle.

Fill in each sentence with the correct word:

Vital   Vivid   Antibiotic   Biography   Biology

1. Andrew realized that having _____ imagination is _____ for success in creative writing class.

2. When he read a George Washington _____ Grant learned that Washington didn't like to smile because his wooden false teeth embarrassed him.

3. Rachel saw unusual plants in the botanical garden and wondered if any of them had _____ properties.

Choose the correct definition:

1. **Biology**
   a. study of logic
   b. a life story
   c. the science of living things
   d. full of life

2. **Vital**
   a. a life story
   b. necessary
   c. a kind of light-giving squid
   d. the science of living things

3. **Biography**
   a. a life story
   b. important for life
   c. a famous actor
   d. the science of living things

4. **Antibiotic**
   a. the science of life
   b. light made by living things
   c. decay or rot
   d. a medicine that kills germs

Make a sentence with each of the following words:

Biology   Vivid   Biography   Antibiotic

Challenge Words, look up these words in the dictionary:

Bionic   Vivacious   Revitalize

Biology teacher: *Can you name six animals that live in the Arctic?*
Student: *Two sea lions and four polar bears.*

HYDR and AQUA

The Greek roots **hydra-** and **hydro-** mean **water**.
The Latin root **aqua-** also means **water**.

Aquatic: living or taking place in water, usually in the sea or ocean
They went snorkeling and saw all kinds of amazing and beautiful <u>aquatic</u> life.
They went snorkeling and saw all kinds of amazing and beautiful <u>oceanic</u> life.

Aquamarine: a pale blue to greenish blue color, like the color of the sea
The water was an <u>aquamarine</u> color, so clear you could see the ocean floor.
The water was a <u>bluish green</u> color, so clear you could see the ocean floor.

Aquarium: a fish tank, a place for the public to look at different fish and sea-life
Johnny loved feeding the fish in his <u>aquarium</u> every day.
Johnny loved feeding the fish in his <u>fish tank</u> every day.

Hydrophobia (*phobia* means fear): an abnormal fear of water
Jesse wouldn't even get on a boat because of his <u>hydrophobia</u>.
Jesse wouldn't even get on a boat because of his <u>fear of water</u>.

Dehydration: loss of water from the body
Two minutes after working in the hot sun, Blair began complaining about <u>dehydration</u>.
Two minutes after working in the hot sun, Blair began complaining about <u>his body losing water</u>.

Tidbit

Aquarius is one of the 12 zodiac star signs and means the "water carrier." In ancient Babylonian and Greek mythology, **Aquarius** was the god of water. He has his own constellation (group of stars) that looks like a stick figure pouring out water onto the stars.
Aquarius is also the name given to the underwater science research center off the coast of Florida. Two scientists can stay underwater inside Aquarius for up to ten days and do all their research. The scientists on the Aquarius often call themselves "aquanauts".

Fill in each sentence with the correct word:

Aquatic   Dehydration   Aquarium   Aquamarine   Hydrophobia

1. Due to her terrible _____ , Elizabeth didn't even want to go near the ocean. After a while, her friends managed to drag her in and she was amazed at all the _____ life that she saw.

2. It took two hours for Hilary to choose a party dress. In the end, she picked one that was an _____ color.

3. The desert tour guide warned us about _____ and advised to drink plenty of water before the tour.

4. Jenny claimed that her cousin Sally keeps a small shark in her_____.

Choose the correct definition:

1. **Aquatic**
   a. blue-green
   b. scared of water
   c. a tank of water
   d. living or being in water

2. **Aquarium**
   a. a fish tank
   b. a zodiac sign
   c. blue-green
   d. scared of water

3. **Aquamarine**
   a. a kind of submarine
   b. a blue-green color
   c. a crayon
   d. living or being in water

4. **Hydrophobia**
   a. a tank of water
   b. fear of water
   c. blue-green
   d. living in water

Make a sentence with each of the following words:

Aquatic   Aquarium   Aquamarine   Dehydration

Challenge Words, look up these words in the dictionary:

Hydraulic   Hydroplane   Aqualung

A person on the beach: Is that your son who buried my clothes in the sand?
The lady: No, that's my nephew. My son made an aquarium out of your hat.

PORT

This root means **carry**.

Porter: a person who carries baggage
The hotel <u>porter</u> took their luggage to Room 626.
The hotel <u>baggage carrier</u> took their luggage to Room 626.

Export: to send out products to another place
California <u>exports</u> cheese to many other parts of the country.
California <u>sends</u> cheese to many other parts of the country.

Deport: to expel from a country, to banish
The court ordered to <u>deport</u> the criminal.
The court ordered to <u>expel</u> the criminal.

Reporter: a writer, investigator, or presenter of news stories
The <u>reporter</u> interviewed the mayor about the election.
The <u>news writer</u> interviewed the mayor about the election.

Transport: to carry or move things from place to place
In Europe, trains are used to <u>transport</u> people from place to place.
In Europe, trains are used to <u>move</u> people from place to place.

Confusion Alert!

The words **import** and **export** are often confused. **Import** means bringing goods into a place, while **export** means the opposite, to send things out.

Tidbit

Exports are goods that are sold and sent elsewhere either out of state or country. The United States is the world's largest **exporting** country, **transporting** almost a trillion dollars worth of goods around the world! Canada is the largest **export** market for the United States. Mexico is second, followed closely by Japan. In the United States, the government controls the **export** of all products and charges special taxes on the imports, called duties or tariff.

Fill in each sentence with the correct word:

Porter   Export   Reporter   Transport

1. The _____ presented a news story about the _____ of fruits to other countries.

2. We thanked the _____ after he carried our heavy bags up the stairs.

3. States with a lot of coal mines are likely to _____ coal to other states.

4. Airplanes are used to _____ people over large distances.

Choose the correct definition:

1. **Transport**
   a. to move across distance
   b. to stand still
   c. to swim the English Channel
   d. to watch trains

2. **Reporter**
   a. a writer of the news
   b. an essay written for school
   c. moves things
   d. a person who carries luggage

3. **Porter**
   a. a writer of the news
   b. a person who carries luggage
   c. a person who stands still
   d. a person who makes pottery

4. **Deport**
   a. to take away baggage
   b. to send a person away
   c. to invite many people
   d. a writer of the news

Make a sentence with each of the following words:

Reporter   Transport   Export   Deport

Challenge Words, look up these words in the dictionary:

Portable   Purport   Support

Customer: *Excuse me sir, the Swiss cheese I bought yesterday, was it **imported** or **deported**?*

CIRC and CIRCUM

These roots mean **round, around**, or **shaped like a ring**.

Circumstance: a condition, situation; event
The police were investigating the circumstances of the theft.
The police were investigating the conditions of the theft.

Circumference: the distance around a circle
The teacher asked the class to measure the circumference of a paper plate.
The teacher asked the class to measure the distance around a paper plate.

Circular: round, made in the shape of a ring
A carpenter used a circular saw to cut the wood.
A carpenter used a round blade to cut the wood.

Circulation: movement of air around the Earth or blood around a body
We can guess the weather by studying the circulation of cold and hot air.
We can guess the weather by studying the round movements of cold and hot air.

Circumvent: to go around
Sid, a careful traveler, chose to circumvent the mountain instead of climbing it.
Sid, a careful traveler, chose to go around the mountain instead of climbing it.

Tidbit

 Ferdinand Magellan, a Portuguese explorer, is famous for **circumnavigating** (going around the globe) in 1520. The voyage proved that the Earth is round, although most educated people of that time knew this already. During the trip, Magellan and his crew discovered and named new lands. Among them was Tierra del Fuego or the Land of Fire. It was named after the crew saw multiple fires made by the natives. Magellan died before the end of the journey and only one of the five ships that started the **circumnavigation** voyage made it back home.

Fill in each sentence with the correct word:

Circumference   Circular   Circulation   Circumvent   Circumstances

1. Jenny promised to show up on time no matter what the _____.

2. Bill will _____ Los Angeles while going south to avoid the traffic.

3. Most clocks have a _____ shape.

4. Many old people have poor _____ because they do not get much exercise.

5. Take your measuring tape and find out the _____ of this wheel.

Choose the correct definition:

1. **Circulation**
   a. movement of air and water around the Earth
   b. flow of blood in the body in circular way
   c. the number of copies of a magazine or newspaper sold or distributed
   d. all the above

2. **Circumstance**
   a. to have walls on all sides   c. a situation
   b. round shape   d. to go around in a ship

3. **Circumvent**
   a. to have walls on all sides   c. to wander around
   b. to look around   d. to go around

4. **Circular**
   a. to walk around   c. to jump around
   b. to look around   d. to be round in shape

Make a sentence with each of the following words:

Circulation   Circumference   Circumvent

Challenge Words, look up these words in the dictionary:

Circa   Circumspect

The roundest knight at King Arthur's round table was Sir Cumference.

CYCL and CYCLO

The Greek roots **cycl** and **cyclo** mean **round**, **circle**, **wheel**, or **spinning**.

Cycle: a circle; a period of time; something happening time after time
Francis watched the cars race around the track in an endless <u>cycle</u>.
Francis watched the cars race around the track in an endless <u>circle</u>.

Cyclone: a tornado, wind blowing in a circle, a twister
Everybody in the Midwest knows what to do when they see a <u>cyclone</u>.
Everybody in the Midwest knows what to do when they see a <u>twister</u>.

Cyclical: regularly, repeated events, moving in a circle
Our weather system is <u>cyclical</u>, the seasons come and go one after another.
Our weather system is <u>repetitive</u>, the seasons come and go one after another.

Recycle: using old materials to make something new, reuse
Don't throw away this empty glass bottle, <u>recycle</u> it.
Don't throw away this empty glass bottle, <u>use it again</u>.

Bicycle: EVERYONE knows what a bicycle is!
Tricycle: this might have been your first.
Unicycle: has one wheel, it takes some skill to ride this one.
Motorcycle: always wear a helmet when riding these.

Tidbit

 In Greek mythology, a **Cyclops** was a giant creature with only one round eye in the middle of its forehead. The **Cyclops** appeared in the Greek epic, *The Odyssey*, a great story of an ancient adventure was written by the blind poet Homer. In this story, the hero Odysseus and his friends get captured by the **Cyclops**, but manage to escape by poking the giant in the eye. The X-Men comic book took the name **Cyclops** and gave it to one of the mutants who could shoot an energy beam from his eye.

Big Words for Little Kids

Fill in each sentence with the correct word:

Cycle   Cyclone   Cyclical   Recycling

1. Jeff saw the dark clouds come together and watched the wind as the
   _____ began to form.

2. By mistake Tammy threw her school yearbook in a _____ bin.

3. The earth has a fixed amount of water. It goes from water to vapor to rain in
   an endless _____ .

4. The harvest seasons repeat so we can call them _____ .

Choose the correct definition:

1. **Cycle**
   a. a two-wheeled vehicle   c. a motorbike
   b. tornado, a twister   d. a circle

2. **Cyclone**
   a. a unicycle   c. a circle
   b. a tornado, a twister   d. a one-eyed monster

3. **Cyclical**
   a. moving in circles   c. likes to spin
   b. a two-wheeled vehicle   d. a selfish person

4. **Recycle**
   a. riding a bicycle again   c. lunch break
   b. using something again   d. moving in circles

Make a sentence with each of the following words:

Cycle   Cyclical   Cyclone   Recycle

Challenge Words, look up these words in the dictionary:

Encyclopedia   Cyclist

*A boy rides a new **bicycle**. "Look mom, no hands." he yells as he turns*
the corner. Five minutes later, he rides back: "Look mom, no tooth!"

MAL

This Latin root means **bad** or **evil**.

Malady: sickness, disease, illness
In May, June had a <u>malady</u> that kept her out of school; in June, May got sick.
In May, June had an <u>illness</u> that kept her out of school; in June, May got sick.

Malice: hatred, meanness, wishing others harm, nastiness
Brent didn't bear any <u>malice</u> for the guest team but wanted them to lose badly anyway.
Brent didn't bear any <u>hatred</u> for the guest team, but wanted them to lose badly anyway.

Malcontent: a person who is not happy with the way things are, a grouch
Everyone says that Dr. Wolff became a <u>malcontent</u> after he retired.
Everyone says that Dr. Wolff became a <u>grouch</u> after he retired.

Malicious: done just to be mean, hateful, nasty
He destoryed my model just to be <u>malicious</u>.
He destoryed my model just to be <u>mean</u>.

Malign: to say (Usually unfairly) bad things about someone
Angry at not being invited to the birthday party, Tina <u>maligned</u> Nina at every chance.
Angry at not being invited to the birthday party, Tina <u>said bad things</u> about Nina at every chance.

Tidbit

The word **malaria** in Italian literally means *bad air*. The root language of Italian, along with languages like French and Spanish, is Latin. Many of these roots, like *mal*, never changed from their original form. Caused by a parasite and carried by mosquitoes, **malaria** used to be a curse of any swampy area in the world. In Africa, **malaria** kills millions of people and is still the leading cause of death for children under five.

Fill in each sentence with the correct word:

Malady   Malice   Malcontent   Malpractice   Maligned

1. James acted like a _____ whenever he stayed home with a _____ ;
   for him either the chicken soup was too hot or the room was too cold.

2. No one spoke to Ron in the play-ground and he wondered if he was being
   _____ by Jill again.

3. It was clearly _____ when the nurse gave the shot to me instead of to
   my sister.

4. George suspected _____ when he saw his beautifully carved pumpkin
   smashed to pieces.

Choose the correct definition:

1. **Malice**
   a. meanness
   b. sickness
   c. badly treated
   d. in Wonderland

2. **Malady**
   a. ill will
   b. good health
   c. sickness, disease
   d. nice music

3. **Malcontent**
   a. meanness, ill will
   b. sickness
   c. bad choice
   d. unhappiness, a grouch

4. **Malign**
   a. to draw a bad line
   b. talk badly about someone
   c. waiting for your turn
   d. to tell lies

Make a sentence with each of the following words:

Malady   Malice   Malcontent   Malign

Challenge Words, look up these words in the dictionary:

Malevolent   Malignant

Luke: *First, I had **malaria**, then appendicitis, then pneumonia, then
sinusitis, and in the end - meningitis.*
Sarah: *How did you survive?*
Luke: *I don't know. That was the worst spelling test of my life.*

VINC and VICT

The Latin roots **vinc-** and **vict-** mean to **win over**, to **defeat** or **conquer**.

Victor: the winner; also name
Mark was the <u>victor</u> over his friend in the one-on-one basketball game.
Mark was the <u>winner</u> over his friend in the one-on-one basketball game.

Victorious: being a winner
In a battle of wits, Ronnie, the genius, was always <u>victorious</u> over the other kids.
In a battle of wits, Ronnie, the genius, was always the a <u>winner</u> over the other kids.

Convict: a criminal (a noun); to find someone guilty of a crime (a verb)
The jury decided to <u>convict</u> burglar Bill for robbing the Quik-Mart.
The jury decided to <u>find</u> burglar Bill <u>guilty</u> of robbing the Quik-Mart.

Convince: get someone to believe something, win over someone in an argument
Julie tried to <u>convince</u> us she was a real princess, even though she was born in Montana.
Julie tried to <u>get</u> us <u>to believe</u> she was a real princess, even though she was born in Montana.

Invincible: unbeatable
Joyce felt <u>invincible</u> in the race as she could run the track faster than everyone.
Joyce felt <u>unbeatable</u> in the race as she could run the track faster than everyone.

Tidbit

The pharaohs, of ancient Egypt thought they would be **victorious** over death by building pyramids and protecting their bodies. Instead of thinking that they would lose all their belongings when they died, they thought they could take all their stuff with them to the place their souls went. The Egyptians were **convinced** they would be **victorious** over death and live among the gods with all of their cool stuff if they turned themselves into mummies.

Fill in each sentence with the correct word (more than one word may fit)

Convict   Convince   Invincible   Victorious

1. Tammy's team was the winner of the soccer tournament. As she stood there holding the trophy, Tammy felt _____.

2. The _____ was sent to jail right after the judge said he was guilty.

3. Michael tried to _____ his coach that it wouldn't take the whole summer of hard training to be _____ in the competition.

4. It took quite a while for Joe to _____ his four-year-old sister that the sun was actually a star.

Choose the correct definition:

1. **Convince**
   a. get someone to believe something   b. the winner
   b. cannot be defeated   d. to accuse someone of a crime

2. **Invincible**
   a. win over verbally   c. unable to be seen
   b. cannot be defeated   d. the winner

3. **Convict**
   a. get someone to believe something   c. to win
   b. force someone out of a house   d. find guilty of a crime

4. **Victorious**
   a. being a winner   c. being a pharaoh
   b. being a loser   d. being there

Make a sentence with each of the following words:

Convince   Convict   Victorious   Invincible

Challenge Words, look up these words in the dictionary:

Evict   Victim

Teacher: *Billy, what do you want to be when you grow up?*
Billy: *A policeman.*
Teacher: *And you, Seth?*
Seth: *A **convict**, so I can still play with Billy.*

FORC and FORT

These roots mean **strong**.

Fort: a stronghold for protection, an army post, a castle
Fortify: to make stronger
Mike wanted to <u>fortify</u> his snow <u>fort</u> with ice but had to settle for cardboard.
Mike wanted to <u>make stronger</u> his snow <u>castle</u> with ice but had to settle for cardboard.

Fortitude: strength of mind and character, guts, courage
She had the <u>fortitude</u> to keep going even when hike path became very steep.
She had the <u>strength of character</u> to keep going even when hike path became very steep.

Force: power, strength, pressure
The physician applied gentle <u>force</u> to her knee to see how badly it was injured.
The physician applied gentle <u>pressure</u> to her knee to see how badly it was injured.

Effort: the use of physical or mental strength to do something
It was a huge <u>effort</u> to get the house ready in time for dad's birthday surprise.
It was a huge <u>act of strength</u> to get the house ready in time for dad's birthday surprise.

Confusion Alert!

The word **fortune** has a similar root and means a chance or luck that doesn't usually come with force. **Fortunate** means having good luck.
One would need to be <u>fortunate</u> to win the lottery.
One would need to have <u>good luck</u> to win the lottery.

Tidbit

 The Alamo is a chapel in San Antonio, Texas that was turned into a **fort**. In 1836, several thousand Mexican soldiers approached the Alamo, which was defended by only 150 Texans. Due to confusion and power struggle among other Texans, almost no support arrived to help defend the Alamo. Refusing to surrender, the Texans in the **fort** were ready to fight until the end. The siege lasted over twelve days, and ended with hand-to-hand fighting within the Alamo's walls. The heroic resistance roused fighting anger among other Texans, and six weeks later the Mexicans army was defeated at San Jacinto to the Texan battle cry of "Remember the Alamo!"

Fill in each sentence with the correct word:

Fort   Force   Effort   Fortitude   Fortunate

1. They made a heroic _____in their last stand at the _____,
    but in the end the weary soldiers lost the battle.

2. We were _____ that support and supplies arrived just in time.

3. Even the enemy was willing to admit the _____ of the soldiers inside
    the_____.The enemy was not so _____ and was defeated
    in the end.

4. _____ Ross is an army post built by the Russians in the 19th century
    on the coast of Northern California near San Francisco.

Choose the correct definition:

1. **Fort**
    a. a stronghold or protection   c. having good luck
    b. power, strength, pressure   d. strength of character

2. **Force**
    a. a stronghold of protection   c. weakness
    b. power, strength, pressure   d. having good luck

3. **Fortunate**
    a. having bad luck   c. a lottery ticket
    b. having good luck   d. weakness

4. **Fortitude**
    a. having good luck   c. strength of character
    b. a stronghold for protection   d. a long battle

Make a sentence with each of the following words:

Force   Fort   Fortitude   Fortify

Challenge Words, look up these words in the dictionary:

Forte   Fortress   Reinforcements

Mom is talking to her son who is studying to become a chef.
Mom: *Do they let you eat the food that you prepare?*
Son: *Let us? They are* **forcing** *us!*

PRO

This prefix means **in front**. It is also has an another meanings, **for** or **forward**. For example, people who are **for** America are called **pro**-American.

Procrastinate: to put off doing something, usually because of laziness; to delay
Mike <u>procrastinated</u> until the last minute before doing his math homework.
Mike <u>put-off</u> until the last minute before doing his math homework.

Procure: to take care, to get something by special effort
Clever James managed to <u>procure</u> free tickets to the rock concert!
Clever James managed to <u>use some special effort to get</u> free tickets to the rock concert!

Proceed: to go forward, to continue, to carry on
During the fire drills, everyone was told to <u>proceed</u> from the building in rows.
During the fire drills, everyone was told to <u>continue</u> out of the building in rows.

Propose: to put forth an idea; to suggest or offer
For the field trip, Darcy <u>proposed</u> a pool party at her house.
For the field trip, Darcy <u>suggested</u> a pool party at her house.

Other words with the prefix **pro**:
Provide: to supply, to make ready ahead of time
Progress: to step forward toward a goal
Prospect: something expected, a possibility, a potential customer

Tidbit

Everyone knows how the usual marriage **proposal** works: the man gets down on his knee, opens a box with a diamond ring in it, and slips it onto the finger of his crying bride-to-be. For the Wodaabe of West Africa, **proposing** is less about jewelry and more about makeup - the man's! During a courtship festival, Wodaabe men put on fancy makeup and costumes and dance for days to impress the women that gather around to watch. If one of the dancing men spots a woman he likes, he can sneak up to her house that night and try to steal her away-even if she's already married! But if the woman doesn't like the thief, she can call her husband or the family to beat him up! You might think the Wodaabe men are lucky because they can skip expensive diamond rings, but at least in America men don't have to run and hide from angry husbands!

Fill in each sentence with the correct word:

Propose   Proceed   Procure   Procrastinate

1. After setting up camp, the next job was to see if they can _____ some firewood from somewhere.

2. Juan decided that if they couldn't find enough wood to have a bonfire on the beach, then they would _____ to have a sing-a-along by candle light.

3. Because Fatima had decided to _____, it was not done well and she was unhappy with it.

Choose the correct definition:

1. **Procrastinate**
   a. to suggest an idea   c. to put forward
   b. to get something   d. to put off, to delay

2. **Procure**
   a. cure from an illness   c. to put off till tomorrow
   b. to get or obtain   d. to make an offer

3. **Proceed**
   a. to go forward, to continue   c. favoring, supporting
   b. to delay, postpone   d. to acquire

4. **Propose**
   a. to put an idea forward   c. to put off
   b. to get married   d. to get by special effort

Make a sentence with each of the following words:

Propose   Proceed   Procure   Procrastinate

Challenge Words, look up these words in the dictionary:

Profess (the word *professor* comes from this word)   Propel

> **Dad:** *Eric, did you* **promise** *to be home at six?*
> **Eric:** *Yes, dad.*
> **Dad:** *And did I* **promise** *to ground you if you were late?*
> **Eric:** *Yes, dad, and since I did not keep my* **promise***, you don't have to keep yours either.*

DE

The prefix **de-** means **from** and **away.**

Destroy: to break, to ruin, to tear down
A powerful wind <u>destroyed</u> our tree house.
A powerful wind <u>broke</u> our tree house.

Deception: a lie, a trick, cheating, a fake
The magician made a lion disappear from the stage by <u>deception</u>.
The magician made a lion disappear from the stage by a <u>trick</u>.

Deprive: to take something away or to keep from getting
The whole class was upset when we were <u>deprived</u> of our lunch break.
The whole class was upset when we our lunch break <u>was taken away</u>.

Determine: to explain, to find out the cause, to make a decision
The scientist have <u>determined</u> that eating veggies makes you taller.
The scientist have <u>found out</u> that eating veggies makes you taller.

Declare: to make it known, to speak out, to announce
The judge was ready to <u>declare</u> her decision.
The judge was ready to <u>announce</u> her decision.

Confusion Alert!

The word **desert** sounds very similar to the word **dessert.** The noun **desert** is an empty, dry, and hot land. The verb **desert** means run away from military without permission.
Dessert, on the other hand, is a sweet food, such as ice cream, cake, or fruit at the end of a meal. If you are in a hurry, eat the dessert first.

Tidbit

Sleep **deprivation** means not getting enough sleep. It can be because of a disease or staying up late at night, as many teenagers do. The studies showed that there are millions of people in the United States who suffer from sleep **deprivation.** Lack of sleep is particularly bad for children because during the sleep the brain sorts out and stores everything that they learned during the day. Sleep **deprivation** makes the wounds heal slower and keeps children from growing tall by holding back growth hormone. So, when my grandmother told me that I was growing while sleeping, she was right!

Big Words for Little Kids

Fill in each sentence with the correct word:

Destroy   Deception   Deprive   Determine   Declared

1. Martin Luther King's Day is _____ a national holiday.

2. I've read that everything in the store was on sale, but that was a _____.

3. Cutting trees will _____ the rain forest and will _____ the animals of a place to live.

4. Sonia spent all evening trying to _____ the real problem with her computer.

Choose the correct definition:

1. **Destroy**
   a. to build
   b. to brake
   c. to break
   d. to trick

2. **Deprive**
   a. to take away
   b. to bring in
   c. to break
   d. a sweet treat

3. **Declare**
   a. a take away
   b. to explain
   c. to speak out
   d. to make a decision

4. **Determine**
   a. to build
   b. to keep from getting
   c. to find out
   d. to run away

Make a sentence with each of the following words:

Destroy   Deprive   Determine   Declare

Challenge Words, look up these words in the dictionary:

Detest   Deform   Debunk   Depose   Deride

Teacher: *Johnny, use defeat, deduct, defense, and detail in one sentence.*
Tommy: *De-feet of De-duck went over De-fence before De-tail.*

UNI

The Latin prefix **uni-** means **one**.

Unique: one of a kind, original
Jared created <u>unique</u> art by gluing together pieces of wood, wire and fabric.
Jared created <u>one of a kind</u> art by gluing together pieces of wood, wire and fabric.

Unison: sounding the same note, being in agreement, or working together as one
The singers in the choir sang in <u>unison</u>, making it sound like they all had one voice.
The singers in the choir <u>sang as one</u>, making it sound like they all had one voice.

Unanimous: total agreement by everyone
The decision to buy chocolate ice cream was <u>unanimous</u>.
The decision to buy chocolate ice cream was <u>the one everybody agreed on</u>.

NOTE: In this word, **uni** is shortened to **un**, but the letter U is still sounds the same as in other "**uni**" words. In the words where the prefix **un** means **not**, the letter U is pronounced like in the word *underwear*.

Unify: to join two or more things together
Roy and Marissa were <u>unified</u> in their opinion that purple is the wrong color for the bedroom ceiling.
Roy and Marissa <u>joined together</u> in their opinion that purple is the wrong color for the bedroom ceiling.

The words **union** and **united** in names like the former Soviet Union and the United States also come from the prefix **uni.**

Tidbit

 The **unicycle** is a bicycle with only one wheel. The unicycle was invented by accident from the *high wheel*, also known as *penny-farthing*, bicycle. This 19th century bike had a huge front wheel and a tiny back wheel. If a rider stopped suddenly, the back wheel would go up into the air. People found that they could ride around with the back wheel in the air for awhile, and so the **unicycle** was invented.

Fill in each sentence with the correct word:

Unison   Unique   Unanimous   Unify

1. Every month Carla has a new and _____ hairstyle. This month it's a bright green Mohawk.

2. Jim's mom always tries to _____ the family by renting a movie that they can all watch together.

3. The entire class was _____ in their decision to have a pool party at the end of the year.

4. The huge choir sang in perfect _____ .

Choose the correct definition:

1. **Unison**
   a. singing in a choir
   b. doing together as one
   c. relating to the whole world
   d. having one son

2. **Unanimous**
   a. everyone agreeing on something
   b. not animate
   c. one animal
   d. disagreement

3. **Unify**
   a. differences
   b. relating to the whole world
   c. take apart
   d. bringing together

4. **Unique**
   a. a kind of bicycle
   b. one of a kind
   c. agreement from everyone
   d. doing something together

Make a sentence with each of the following words:

Unique   Unison   Unanimous   Unity

Challenge Words, look up these words in the dictionary:

Unilateral   Uniform   Universal

The boys tells his father about the movie he watched.
The boy: *And then the monster cries"ahhhh", and the bad guy screams "oh no!"*
Dad: *Please, start from the beginning.*
The boy, *with a sigh: **Universal** Studios presents...*

BI

The prefix **bi-** means **two**.

Bilateral: having two sides or affecting two sides evenly; two-way
Despite the tall fence between our houses, we have a good <u>bilateral</u> relationship with our neighbors.
Despite the tall fence between our houses we have a good <u>two-way</u> relationship with our neighbors.

Bilingual: able to speak two languages
Maria was <u>bilingual</u> and often translated for her Spanish speaking grandma.
Maria was <u>able to speak two languages</u> and often translated for her Spanish speaking grandma.

Bisect: to cut into two equal parts, to split in half
Draw a triangle. Now draw a line that <u>bisects</u> it.
Draw a triangle. Now draw a line that <u>cuts it in half</u>.

Bipedal: an animal that walks on two feet
Gorilla are <u>bipedal</u> and can walk upright, but their bodies are built differently than ours so it's more comfortable for them to hunch over.
Gorilla are <u>animals with two walking feet</u> and can walk upright, but their bodies are built differently than ours so it's more comfortable for them to hunch over.

There are a lot of common words that start with Latin prefix **bi**, like **bicycle** and **binoculars**. Do you know the others?
Biathlon: a winter Olympic sport that combines skiing and target shooting
Biweekly: once every two weeks, or twice in one week.
Bimonthly: once every two months, or twice in one month.
Biannually or **biennially**: once every two years, or twice in one year.
What do you think **bicentennial** means? Hint: the word century means 100 years.

Tidbit

 Faith, a 19-month-old Labrador-Chow mix, is a pretty amazing **bipedal** dog. She was born without fully formed front legs. When a veterinarian took them off because they had become useless, her Oklahoma family decided to teach her how to walk anyway! Over the course of six months, the family taught her to stand, hop, and eventually walk and run on her two back legs. They even put her on a skateboard! Today she's a happy, healthy **biped** who runs around like a person!

Fill in each sentence with the correct word:

Bisect   Bilateral   Bipedal   Bilingual   Bicycle

1. Because Andrea was _____, she sometimes spoke the wrong language when she got excited.

2. Jared always thought it was a good thing he was _____, or he'd have a tough time riding his _____.

3. Darren could never eat spaghetti normally, he had to _____ each noodle and then eat the two parts separately.

4. Manju and Mina did not talk to each other for three months, so their friends went through a _____ negotiation to bring them together.

Choose the correct definition:

1. **Bilateral**
   a. having two legs
   b. a two wheeled vehicle
   c. having two sides
   d. having two angles

2. **Bilingual**
   a. having two feet
   b. to divide into two parts
   c. able to speak two languages
   d. having two ears

3. **Bipedal**
   a. an animal with two feet
   b. pedaling with both feet
   c. able to speak two languages
   d. to divide in half

4. **Bisect**
   a. to divide into two equal parts
   b. two kinds of insects
   c. knowing two languages
   d. an insect with only two legs

Challenge Words, look up these words in the dictionary:

Bimanual   Bipolar

*The **bicycle** couldn't stand on its own because it was two-tired.*

MONO

The Greek prefix **mono-** means **one**.

Monolith (lith means rock): a large stone often used for sculptures
The 100-foot statue of Buddha in Afghanistan was carved out of a <u>monolith</u>.
The 100-foot statue of Buddha in Afghanistan was carved out of a <u>large rock</u>.

Monopoly (poly means to sell): a complete control, mostly on making and selling things
Jenna talked as if she had a <u>monopoly</u> on good taste in clothes. Excuse me!
Jenna talked as she had <u>total control</u> on good taste in clothes. Excuse me!

Monogram (gram means letter): symbol of a name created from a person's initials
Without thinking, Brad Odly put his <u>monogram</u> BO on all his clothes.
Without thinking, Brad Odly put a BO <u>symbol</u> on all his clothes.

Monograph: a book or an article written about one subject
Celia wrote a <u>monograph</u> on bullying, because she always got picked on.
Celia wrote an <u>article about one subject</u> – bullying, because she always got picked on.

Monologue (log means talk): a long talk made by one person
Kim wanted to talk with Frank, not to listen to his endless <u>monologue</u>.
Kim wanted to talk with Frank, not to listen to him <u>blab on and on by himself</u>.

Tidbit

A **monocle**, meaning *one eye*, is an eye glass for one eye only. It is made of one wire-ringed lens with a string attached on one side. **Monocles** first appeared in Europe in 1830's and were very popular for almost a century. Men with monocles thought they looked so handsome! Several fictional characters have worn monocles, such as The Penguin from the Batman comics. People do not wear monocles any more. Those who need eye correction in just one eye usually choose to wear a single contact lens instead.

Big Words for Little Kids

Fill in each sentence with the correct word:

Monograph   Monogram   Monologues

1. The playwriter was famous for the powerful _____ she gave to the main characters.

2. Every shirt in his closet was carefully folded and had a _____ on the left cuff.

3. Professor Pigeon's _____ on city birds was most informative.

Choose the correct definition:

1. **Monolith**
   a. a symbol made up of initials
   b. a book written on one subject
   c. a long talk by one person
   d. a big solid stone

2. **Monologue**
   a. a symbol made up of initials
   b. a book written on one subject
   c. a long talk by one person
   d. a solid stone

3. **Monograph**
   a. a symbol made up of initials
   b. a book written on one subject
   c. a long talk by one person
   d. exclusive control to sell goods

4. **Monogram**
   a. a symbol made up of initials
   b. a book written on one subject
   c. a long talk by one person
   d. exclusive control to sell goods

Make a sentence with each of the following words:

Monograph   Monolith   Monopoly   Monogram   Monologue

Challenge Words, look up these words in the dictionary:

Monotony   Monochrome

*A boy enters a toy store and hands $100 **Monopoly** game money to the sales lady.*
Boy: *I want to buy a stuffed tiger.*
Sales lady: *But this money is not real!*
Boy: *But neither is the tiger...*

OMNI

The Latin prefix **omni-** means **all** or **everything**.

Omnipresent: universal, present everywhere at the same time
Traveling around the world, Ian noticed that McDonald's restaurants were omnipresent.
Traveling around the world, Ian noticed that McDonald's restaurants were everywhere.

Omnipotent: all-powerful, invincible, often in reference to God or gods
Many believed that Alexander the Great was omnipotent because he did not lose a single battle.
Many believed that Alexander the Great was all-powerful and invincible because he did not lose a single battle.

Omniscient: all-knowing, having entire knowledge
My mother is omniscient because she knows what I'm doing even when she's not around.
My mother is all-knowing because she knows what I'm doing even when she's not around.

Omnivorous: animals that eat both animals and plants
Dogs are omnivorous, but rabbits are not.
Dogs eat both animals and plants, but rabbits do not.

Tidbit

Pigs are very interesting **omnivorous** animals. They eat pretty much everything that humans eat, and that means they can eat a lot! In the wild, pigs eat mushrooms, leaves, roots, bulbs, fruit, snails, earthworms, small animals, dead animals, eggs, and whatever else they can find. They use their strong, muscular snout and feet to dig and scratch for food. Pigs are also very smart. Because pigs don't sweat, they have no way to get cool except to roll around in the mud to keep from getting too hot.

Fill in each sentence with the correct word:

Omnivorous   Omniscient   Omnipotent   Omnipresent

1. Don knew the spring was coming by the _____ daffodils and crocus that were blooming through the snow.

2. Tara felt powerful, strong, and _____ whenever she hit a homerun.

3. While Tyler was _____, eating everything on his plate, his vegetarian sister would only eat the vegetables.

4. Cody often wondered if her science teacher was _____ because she seemed to know an answer for every question.

Choose the correct definition:

1. **Omnipresent**
   a. eating both animals and plants
   b. present everywhere at once
   c. a huge birthday present
   d. a kind of pig

2. **Omnipotent**
   a. everywhere at one time
   b. the entire knowledge
   c. both plants and animals
   d. all-powerful, invincible

3. **Omniscient**
   a. all-knowing
   b. invincible
   c. eating both plants and animals
   d. everywhere at once

4. **Omnivorous**
   a. all-powerful
   b. eats both plants and animals
   c. everywhere
   d. knowing everything

Make a sentence with each of the following words:

Omnipresent   Omnipotent   Omniscient   Omnivorous

Challenge Words, look up these words in the dictionary:

Omnificent   Omnibus

> *Little girl walks into a pet store.*
> **Girl:** *I want to buy a rabbit.*
> **Salesman:** *Would you like this cute gray bunny with big eyes or maybe that white and fluffy one with big ears?*
> **Girl:** *It doesn't matter. My pet python is **omnivorous**.*

MACRO and MICRO

The Greek prefix **macro-** means **large**, while **micro-** means **small**.

Microphone (*phone* means sound): a device that makes a normal voice louder
The professor had a quiet voice and used a <u>microphone</u> when speaking to the students.
The professor had a quiet voice and used <u>a device that made her voice louder</u> when speaking to the students.

Microbe: is a small live organism, a germ
There are millions of <u>microbes</u> living in our body.
There are millions of <u>germs</u> living in our body.

Microscope: a tool to see things that are too small to be seen by naked eye
The water looked clean, but under a <u>microscope</u> we could see all kinds of things floating and swimming in it.
The water looked clean, but under a <u>device that made things look bigger</u> we could see all kinds of things floating and swimming in it.

Macrophage (*phage* means to eat); a large cell in the body that eats enemy cells like microbes
When you get sick, your <u>macrophages</u> help you get well again.
When you get sick, your <u>special large cells that eat the microbes</u> help you get well again.

Other words with prefixes macro and micro:
Microcar: a very tiny car.
Microwave: an oven that quickly warms up food.
Microcephaly: a very small head.
Macrodont: having large teeth.

Tidbit

The word **microscope** is made up of two Greek words: *micro*, which means *small*, and *scopos*, which means *to watch*. You've probably seen or used a light **microscope** in science. You put something with **microscopic** material in it on a small glass plate called slide. Then you stick it under the **microscope** and you can see things at 40 times their normal size. Things that are invisible to the human eye are suddenly huge! But there are even bigger **microscopes** out there that can enlarge the objects to 200,000 times the normal size!

Fill in each sentence with the correct word:

Macrophage   Microbes   Microscope   Microphone

1. One _____ can kill hundreds of germs in your body.

2. Mr. Gill, the principle, took the _____ and his booming voice filled the hallways.

3. Even though a hair looks smooth and straight, under the _____ it shows jagged edges that don't look like hair at all!

4. The pediatrician said to take an antibiotic medicine because some dangerous _____ had made him sick.

Choose the correct definition:

1. **Macrophage**
   a. having large teeth
   b. an enlargement device
   c. a small germ
   d. a large cell that eats germs

2. **Microscope**
   a. makes things look smaller
   b. makes things look larger
   c. a small car
   d. a voice magnifier

3. **Microphone**
   a. a very small telephone
   b. a voice magnifier
   c. too small to be seen
   d. a large cell

4. **Microbe**
   a. a small housecoat
   b. a voice magnifier
   c. a germ
   d. a large cell

Make a sentence with each of the following words:

Microscopic   Microphone   Microbe

Challenge Words, look up these words in the dictionary:

Microclimate   Microcosm (hint: *cosmos* means universe)

On a cruise ship in the middle of the night a boy runs around screaming: "Help! Is there a doctor on the ship?! Is there a doctor?" From one of the cabins a sleepy person in pajamas comes out: "I am a doctor, who needs help?"
Boy: *Me. Doctor, what's a seven-letter word for germ?*

ASTER or ASTRO

These roots mean **star**.

Astronomy: science of the heavenly bodies, stars
From a young age, Jake loved <u>astronomy</u>.
From a young age, Jake loved <u>the science of stars</u>.

Astronaut (*naut* means sailor): a space traveler
The <u>astronaut</u> wore a special suit so he could breathe in outer space.
The <u>space traveler</u> wore a special suit so he could breathe in outer space.

Astrology: studying stars as if they influence people's lives
<u>Astrology</u> relies on the position of stars to try to tell the future.
The <u>study of stars</u> looks at the position of those stars to try to tell the future.

Asterisk: *, a tiny star, used in print to note something special
The <u>asterisk</u> means that there is a footnote at the bottom of the page. *
The <u>tiny star</u> means that there is a footnote at the bottom of the page.

Other words with the roots aster and astro:

Asteroid (suffix *oid* means shaped like, resembling): shaped like a star

Astrocyte (*cyte* means cell): a cell in the form of a star

Disaster (*dis* means not): not having lucky stars, bad fortune

Tidbit

In 1961, President Kennedy decided that the United States should send **astronauts** to the moon and back. This started the *Apollo* space program which was the largest scientific project at the time. On June 20, 1969, American **astronauts** Neil Armstrong and Buzz Aldrin stepped onto the moon, while a third **astronaut**, Michael Collins, orbited the moon in the *Apollo 11* command ship. Upon becoming the first person to step onto the moon, Armstrong spoke the famous words, "That's one small step for a man, one giant leap for mankind."

* Footnote goes here.

Fill in each sentence with the correct word:

Astronomy   Astrology   Astronaut   Asterisk

1. _____ is a fascinating science about the positions, movements, and energies of planets, stars, black holes, and other celestial bodies.

2. On the other hand, _____ is a false 'science' that tries to tell a person's future by the position of stars in the sky.

3. The _____ the end of the sentence drew his attention to the author's note on the bottom of the page.

4. The nervous _____ put his helmet on backwards.

Choose the correct definition:

1. **Astronomy**
   a. a space traveler
   b. science of space and the heavenly bodies

2. **Astrology**
   a. science of the heavenly bodies
   b. study of the stars as if they influence events

3. **Astronaut**
   a. science of the heavenly bodies   c. a tiny printed star
   b. a space traveler   d. an underwater traveler

4. **Asterisk**
   a. a space traveler   c. a tiny star
   b. science of the heavenly bodies   d. taking a chance in space

Make a sentence with each of the following words:

Astronaut   Astrology   Astronomy   Asterisk

Challenge Words, look up these words in the dictionary:

Astronomical   Astrograph

First kid: *looking over the shoulder of his friend: I know what your secret password is.*
Second kid: *OK, what is it?*
First kid: *Four asterisks!*

CAPIT and CAPT

The Latin roots **capit** and **capt** mean **head**, **chief**, or **leader**.

Captain: the head, chief, or leader
Sandy was <u>captain</u> of the school's soccer team.
Sandy was <u>head</u> of the school's soccer team.

Decapitate: cut off someone's head
Joel's sister screamed when she saw him <u>decapitate</u> her Barbie doll.
Joel's sister screamed when she saw him <u>chop off the head of</u> her Barbie doll.

Capitulate: to surrender, give up
He finally <u>capitulated</u> and agreed to do the job my way.
He finally <u>gave up</u> and agreed to do the job my way.

Capital: a city that is the center of government or industry; money that's used by a person or company to make more money; the first letter at the beginning of sentences or names
Silicon Valley is considered the computer <u>capital</u> of the world.
Silicon Valley is considered the <u>center</u> of the computer world.

Remember to write Silicon Valley with <u>capital</u> letters!

Confusion Alert!

Don't confuse **capital** with the word **capitol**, which is the *building* where governments do business.

Tidbit

Edward Teach, better known as Black Beard, was the most famous pirate **captain**. He got his nickname because of the long black beard that he wore in pigtails with colored ribbons on the ends. Teach knew that the scarier he looked, the more likely it was that others would **capitulate** to him. During battles, he would put slow burning cords under his beard to create a cloud of smoke around his head. Black Beard was killed in battle in 1718. To warn other pirates, the commander Robert Maynard had Black Beard **decapitated** and hung his head on the front of his ship!

Fill in each sentence with the correct word:

Captain   Decapitate   Capital   Capitulate

1. As _____ of the football team, Pat saw that it was his duty to publicly _____ the tiger mascot that his team stole from the rival school.

2. The chess match took so long that Cameron chose to _____ and go home rather than go on.

3. Jen prides herself in knowing the _____ of every state.

4. We had talents, energy, and free time to start a new videogame company. The only thing lacking was the _____ to pay for it.

Choose the correct definition:

1. **Captain**
   a. a pirate
   b. a center of government
   c. to surrender
   d. the chief or leader

2. **Decapitate**
   a. to cut the head off
   b. to hang on a ship
   c. to take off a cap
   d. to surrender

3. **Capital**
   a. the center of government
   b. the head or chief
   c. Silicon Valley
   d. a kind of computer

4. **Capitulate**
   a. to cut the head off
   b. to surrender or give in
   c. the head or chief
   d. the center of government

Make a sentence with each of the following words:

Captain   Decapitate   Capital   Capitulate

A cruise ship is passing a small island in the Pacific Ocean and one of the passengers asks the captain: Sir, who is that bearded man screaming and waving wildly at us?
Captain: *I don't know madam, but every time we pass by this island, he goes mad!*

OPER

The root **oper-** means **work**.

Operate: to labor, function, or work; to perform surgery
Sean had fun learning how to <u>operate</u> the lasers that doctors use to <u>operate</u> on patients.
Sean had fun learning how to <u>work</u> the lasers that doctors use to <u>perform</u> <u>surgery</u> on patients.

Cooperate: to work together
Two people must really <u>cooperate</u> to win a three-legged race.
Two people must really <u>work together</u> to win a three-legged race.

Operational: working, running, functional
It was lucky that they found an <u>operational</u> drinking fountain on such a hot day.
It was lucky that they found a <u>working</u> drinking fountain on such a hot day.

Operator: a worker who runs a machine
The roller coaster <u>operator</u> let Sharon ride free.
The roller coaster <u>worker who was running the ride</u> let Sharon ride free.

Opera: a play set to music and singing
Donovan neither liked nor understood the <u>opera</u> but felt it would be best not to mention it during the interview.
Donovan neither liked nor understood the <u>play set to music and singing</u> but felt it would be best not to mention it during the interview.

Tidbit

The word **opera** means "work" in Italian. **Opera** is a play set to music. Many famous composers tried their talents in **opera**: Mozart, Beethoven, Tchaikovsky, and many others. In **opera**, instead of speaking the characters sing. **Opera** brings together many talents: an exciting storytelling, beautiful voices, creative costumes, colorful decorations, original dances, and even special effects. That made someone say: "**Opera** is when a guy gets stabbed in the back and instead of bleeding, he sings."

Fill in each sentence with the correct word:

Operate   Cooperate   Operational   Operator

1. Unfortunately for the people stuck on the Ferris wheel, the wheel _____ wasn't sure how to get them down.

2. When the police showed up and saw the ride was not _____, they decided to _____ with the fire department who used a big ladder truck to help get them down.

3. During the rescue operation one firefighter was injured and they had to _____ on his knee the same day.

Choose the correct definition:

1. **Operate**
   a. a worker who runs a machine
   b. to work together
   c. to work a machine
   d. to sing in an opera

2. **Cooperate**
   a. to work together
   b. surgical
   c. a worker
   d. to function

3. **Operational**
   a. to work together
   b. not working
   c. a person who runs a machine
   d. working

4. **Operator**
   a. a person who runs a machine
   b. to work together
   c. a children's rhyme
   d. not working

Make a sentence with each of the following words:

Operate   Cooperate   Operational   Operator

Challenge Words, look up these words in the dictionary:

Operation   Inoperable

*The Italians are known for their love of **opera**. An American **opera** singer was performing in an Italian theater and the crowd kept calling her back to sing again and again. Finally, pleased but tired, she begged: "How many more times do you want me to sing?" And a voice from the crowd came: "Until you get it right!"*

AUTO

The prefix **auto-** means **self, without outside help**.

Automatic: a device that works by itself; done without thinking
I wish this <u>automatic</u> tea maker would also do the dishes.
I wish this tea maker that <u>works by itself</u> would also do the dishes.

Autograph: someone's handwritten signature
The famous player put his <u>autograph</u> on Sam's baseball card.
The famous player put his <u>signature</u> on Sam's baseball card.

Autobiography: a person's own life story
Julie decided that she needed to live a little more before writing her <u>autobiography</u>.
Julie decided that she needed to live a little more before writing her <u>story</u>.

Autocrat (*crat* means power): a dictator, tyrant, or oppressor
Our class president acts like an <u>autocrat</u> and never listens to what others want.
Our class president acts like a <u>tyrant</u> and never listens to what others want.

Confusion Alert!

The prefix **auto-** can be easily confused with the root **auth** which means original or creator. There are several important words that use the root **auth**, such as **author**.

Authentic: real, something that can be believed; genuine and original
At first I doubted that Picasso's painting on Frank's wall was <u>authentic</u>.
At first I doubted that Picasso's painting on Frank's wall was <u>original and real</u>.

Authority: the right to command, power; a person with power
A school principal has the <u>authority</u> to cancel the lunch break.
A school principal has the <u>power</u> to cancel the lunch break.

Tidbit

Autopilot is a device that guides a car or an airplane without help of a human. It is also used for ships and boats. The first **autopilot** was developed in 1912, only 9 years after the famous Wright brothers' flight at Kitty Hawk. This **autopilot** was simple but allowed the plane to fly in chosen direction at a straight line. Modern **autopilots** use computer software. They can follow a complex course, avoid storm areas, and save fuel.

Fill in each sentence with the correct word:

Automatic   Authentic   Autograph   Autocrat

1. Kim stood in line for hours to get an_____ _____from the movie star.

2. The student body president was an _____: she would never let anybody talk during meetings and wouldn't use anybody's ideas but her own.

3. Ari had done ballet for so long that he didn't even have to think about many of his movements, they were _____ .

Choose the correct definition:

1. **Automatic**
   a. a signature
   b. works by itself

   b. a dictator
   d. a person with power

2. **Autograph**
   a. a signature
   b. works by itself

   b. a dictator
   d. a person with power

3. **Autocrat**
   a. a signature
   b. works by itself

   b. a dictator
   d. a person with power

4. **Authority**
   a. signature
   b. works by itself

   b. a dictator
   d. a person with power

Make a sentence with each of the following words:

Automatic   Autobiography   Autograph   Autocrat

Challenge Words, look up these words in the dictionary:

Autopsy   Autonomy

*At the gas station, a little girl asks: When a small **automobile** eats a lot of gas, does it grow up to become a bus?*

PERI

Greek prefix **peri-** means **around** or **surrounding**.

Perimeter: the outer border or edge around an area
The Millers decided to put a white picket fence on the <u>perimeter</u> of their land.
The Millers decided to put a white picket fence <u>around the edge</u> their land.

Periphery: the outside edge of an area, away from the center
The Millers moved to the <u>periphery</u> of the town to live close to the country.
The Millers moved <u>away from the center</u> of town to live close to the country.

The expression **"peripheral vision"** describes the ability to see out of the corner of one's eye, without looking directly at the object.

Pericardium (cardio means heart): lining around the heart
Cardiologist told my grandpa that his <u>pericardium</u> was swollen.
Cardiologist told my grandpa that his <u>heart lining</u> was swollen.

Periscope: a looking device used to see objects that are above of sight, usually seen in submarines
The boys built a <u>periscope</u> to peak into neighbor's back yard without being seen.
The boys built a <u>device to let them see things that are above sight</u> to peak into the neighbor's back yard without being seen.

Tidbit

One of the first submarines (*sub* means under, *marine* means sea) built by the Navy was called the *USS Holland*. Even though the submarine had all kinds of new technologies and improvements, it had one big problem - they couldn't see when they were underwater! The only way to see was to go to the surface and look out of windows. Luckily, Johannes Gutenberg, the inventor of the printing press, developed a **periscope** 500 years earlier. **periscope** (the root *scope* means to look) was an instrument that used a series of mirrors to help pilgrims see over the heads of the crowds. In 1900 it was used to see outside the sub. Now, the **periscope** is the submarine's only way to see the surface while underwater.

Fill in each sentence with the correct word:

Perimeter   Periphery   Periscope   Peripheral

1. Victor spotted a fox in his _____ vision, but by the time he turned his head, it was gone.

2. Every morning Abbey runs laps around the _____ of the schoolyard to train for races.

3. Maria took a tour of the old submarine and even got to look through its _____.

4. Ali knew that he should be happy just to get a new computer, but he also wanted the _____ stuff: the printer and the speakers.

Choose the correct definition:

1. **Perimeter**
   a. the border or edge around an area   b. important stuff
   b. unimportant, minor   d. a submarine

2. **Periphery**
   a. secondary, unimportant   c. an instrument in a submarine
   b. away from the center   d. the border of an area

3. **Periscope**
   a. to see out of the corner of your eye   c. a submarine
   b. a looking device   d. the outside of an area

4. **Peripheral**
   a. an instrument in a submarine   c. good table manners
   b. a border   d. away from the center

Make a sentence with each of the following words:

Perimeter   Periphery   Periscope   Peripheral

Challenge Words, look up these words in the dictionary:

Perinatal (hint: natal means birth)   Period   Peripatetic

Q: *What can fly on the bottom of the ocean?*
A: *A mosquito inside a* **submarine**.

DIS

The prefix **dis-** means **not**.

Discourage: to take away hope; bring someone down; lose courage
The coach felt <u>discouraged</u> after his team lost the first five games.
The coach <u>lost hope</u> after his team lost the first five games.

Disgusting: lack of taste, gross, nasty, unpleasant
Jason thought it was <u>disgusting</u> when Tom blew his nose and wiped it with his sleeve.
Jason thought it was <u>gross and nasty</u> when Tom blew his nose and wiped it with his sleeve.

Discount: a price cut, lower price
Jessica was happy to buy the book of her favorite author at a <u>discount</u>.
Jessica was happy to buy the book of her favorite author at a <u>lower price</u>.

Dishonest: not honest, lying
When asked who broke the vase, Kyle was <u>dishonest</u> and said his brother did it.
When asked who broke the vase, Kyle <u>lied</u> and said his brother did it.

Dissatisfied: not satisfied, unhappy, frustrated
James was <u>dissatisfied</u> that they did not pick him for the team.
James was <u>unhappy</u> that they did not pick him for the team.

Confusion Alert!
Distraction means pulling attention away in another direction.
Noisy TV caused a <u>distraction</u> and I couldn't focus on my homework.
Destruction means ruining, damaging, and breaking.
One of the mayor's duties is to protect the historic monuments from <u>destruction</u>.

Tidbit

Some people feel **discomfort**, nausea, and dizziness when traveling in cars. Sea travel can also cause motion sickness. The cause of motion sickness can be found in the inner ear, an organ inside your ear that's about the size of a pencil eraser that helps you figure out where your body is. There is fluid pressure on the tiny hairs and cells in your inner ear that help you keep your balance as you move. When you're rocking, however, the fluid pressure in the inner ear can change rapidly, confusing the little hair cells. Not reading, avoiding large meals, and choosing a seat that faces forward might help prevent motion sickness while traveling in a car.

Big Words for Little Kids

Fill in each sentence with the correct word:

Discouraged   Dishonest   Disgusting   Discount

1. Sam thought it was _____ the way Dianne chewed her food with the mouth wide open.

2. Darren walked off the stage _____ because he had made so many mistakes during his piano recital.

3. My grandma told me not to buy anything for full price what I can get cheaper with a _____.

4. Brad wasn't really _____, he just liked to brag a little to his friends.

Choose the correct definition:

1. **Dishonest**
   a. not knowing where you are
   b. not comfortable
   c. not happy
   d. not truthful

2. **Dissatisfied**
   a. not comfortable
   b. not satisfied, unhappy
   c. an organ in the inner ear
   d. not oriented

3. **Disgusting**
   a. not happy
   b. not comfortable
   c. bad taste
   d. not honest

4. **Disoriented**
   a. not knowing where you are
   b. not satisfied
   c. not honest
   d. not comfortable

Make a sentence with each of the following words:

Disoriented   Discomfort   Dissatisfied   Dishonest

Challenge Words, look up these words in a dictionary:

Disorganized   Disappointed

Mom walks in and finds her daughter searching through her purse.
Mom: *I am **disappointed** that you are looking inside someone else's purse.*
The daughter: *Mom, why do you have someone else's purse?*

CRED

The root **cred-** means **believe**.

Credible: something believable, reliable, likely, or sincere
Jacob got the news about Lizzie from a <u>credible</u> source: her mother.
Jacob got the news about Lizzie from a <u>believable</u> source: her mother.

Incredible: unbelievable, amazing
James' magic trick was <u>incredible</u>.
James' magic trick was <u>amazing</u>.

Credulous: believing in things easily, gullible, trusting
Jack is so <u>credulous</u> that he believes everything he hears.
Jack is so <u>gullible and trusting</u> that he believes everything he hears.

Credence: acceptance, support; believe
The teacher gave <u>credence</u> to Lily's idea that there once may have been flowing water on Mars.
The teacher gave <u>acceptance and support</u> to Lily's idea that there once may have been flowing water on Mars.

Creditor: a person to whom one owes money or from whom one borrows
My little sister is my <u>creditor,</u> she always has money.
My little sister is the <u>person from whom I borrow money,</u> she always has money.

Tidbit

The Loch Ness Monster, called Nessie by locals of the Loch Ness Lake in Scotland, is an **incredible** mystery. People say that Nessie has always lived the lake but hides most of the time. Many people come to the lake just to see if they can spot him. Despite many **incredible** reports and fuzzy pictures of the 50-foot long creature swimming in the lake, no one has ever found the animal. Many people think it's just a hoax, and that you'd have to be **incredibly credulous** to believe it exists. Others swear that they've seen this monster and have even taken pictures of it.

Fill in each sentence with the correct word:

Credible   Incredible   Creditor   Credulous   Credence

1. Sonia was so _____ that other kids made her believe that the moon was made out of cheese.

2. The way the huge fireworks display lit up the entire night sky and turned night into day was _____.

3. Nobody thought it was_____ when Julie said that snakes used their tongues to smell. However, the science teacher gave _____ to her story.

4. Jimmie's uncle, a millionaire, refused to be his _____ .

Choose the correct definition:

1. **Credible**
   a. amazing
   b. simple
   c. believable and likely
   d. authority

2. **Incredible**
   a. agreement
   b. unbelievable, amazing
   c. a hero
   d. believable

3. **Credence**
   a. acceptance and support
   b. trusting
   c. a rock group
   d. unbelievable

4. **Credulous**
   a. lender
   b. authority
   c. amazing
   d. believes things easily

Make a sentence with each of the following words:

Credible   Incredible   Credence   Credulous

Challenge Words, look up these words in the dictionary:

Incredulous   Discredit

A proud mom tells a guest about her daughter's **incredible** *artistic talent.*
The **incredulous** *guest turns to the girl: Can you draw a cup of coffee?*
The girl: *With or without sugar?*

FER

This root means **bring**, **bear**, or **yield**.

Fertile: producing plenty of food
The fertile farmland bore a huge crop of corn.
The fruitful farmland bore a huge crop of corn.

Conference: a bringing together, a meeting
Amanda had a conference with the other teachers.
Amanda had a meeting with other the teachers.

Suffer: to hurt, to bear sadness or pain
Michael hated watching any movies that showed people suffering.
Michael hated watching any movies that showed people feeling sadness or pain.

Transfer: to move from one place to another
Jill transferred the computer from her home to her office.
Jill moved the computer from her home to her office.

Infer: to conclude or decide, to understand, to figure out
From Susan's guilty look and chocolate-covered face I inferred that she ate the cake.
From Susan's guilty look and chocolate-covered face I figured out that she ate the cake.

Refer: to direct, guide, send; to mention
I asked my brother a science question but he referred me to my dad.
I asked my brother a science question but he sent me to my dad.

Tidbit

The **circumference** is the line that goes around a circle. You can figure out the exact length of a circle's **circumference** if you know the distance between the center of the circle and its outside edge, called the radius. As the radius gets bigger, so does the circumference. Try drawing a few circles of different sizes and see how the radius and circumference are related.

Fill in each sentence with the correct word:

Inferred   Suffering   Transfer   Refer

1. My regular doctor wasn't sure what was wrong with my skin and decided to _____ me to a rash specialist .

2. From their mysterious looks I _____ that they were putting together a surprise party.

3. To get from one end of town to the other, Joe had to _____ from one bus to another several times.

4. The television special showed the _____ of people in war-torn countries.

Choose the correct definition:

1. **Conference**
   a. to agree
   b. to fence off
   c. a meeting or bringing together
   d. to move from one place to another

2. **Fertile**
   a. to agree
   b. bearing plentifully
   c. a type of floor
   d. to guide

3. **Refer**
   a. to agree
   b. to direct
   c. an umpire
   d. a meeting

4. **Transfer**
   a. to agree
   b. to guide
   c. to move from one place to another
   d. a meeting

Make a sentence with each of the following words:

Transfer   Conference   Suffer   Infer

Challenge Words, look up these words in the dictionary:

Odoriferous (hind: odor means smell)   Reference

Son: *Mom, don't you realize that your fur coat is the result of the* ***suffering*** *of a poor, innocent creature?*
Mom: *How dare you to talk like that about your father!*

LOC

The Latin root **loc** means **place**.

Locate: to find a place or person
Jean couldn't <u>locate</u> her homework anywhere, so she figured the dog ate it.
Jean couldn't <u>find</u> her homework anywhere, so she figured the dog ate it.

Dislocate: to move out of place or position
When Pat crashed while skiing, he <u>dislocated</u> his shoulder and had to miss the rest of the season.
When Pat crashed while skiing, his shoulder was <u>moved out of joint</u> and he had to miss the rest of the season.

Allocate: to set aside for special reasons; to give out
Sophie <u>allocated</u> half of her birthday money for buying clothes.
Sophie <u>set aside</u> half of her birthday money for buying clothes.

Relocate: to move to a new place
Every year, thousands of military families <u>relocate</u> after finishing their tours of duty.
Every year, thousands of military families <u>move to a new place</u> after finishing their tours of duty.

Location: a place, site, position
She asked me what was my <u>location</u> and I didn't know what to say.
She asked me <u>where I was</u> and I didn't know what to say.

Tidbit

A lot of cars now come equipped with a GPS, or Global Positioning System. The GPS is a space-based system that tells you your **location**. It costs our government $750 million each year to maintain the system! GPS not only helps **locate** the position of your car so you can get directions, but it is also a useful tool in making maps, studying earthquakes, and aiding the military. But that's not all: GPS helps Minnesota scientists follow the movements and feeding habits of deer, and even shows scientists that Mount Everest, the tallest mountain in the world, is growing!

Fill in each sentence with the correct word:

Locate   Allocate   Dislocate   Relocate

1. In order to get out of a straight jacket, Houdini, a famous magician, had to _____ his shoulder.

2. Oren tried to _____ his friends at the fair, but couldn't find them.

3. A secret agent was forced to _____ every week so that he wouldn't get caught by the enemy.

4. Mrs. Sanchez decided to _____ one-half of her property to the Red Cross.

Choose the correct definition:

1. **Locate**
   a. to assign a place
   b. to find the place
   c. the center of things
   d. a GPS unit

2. **Allocate**
   a. to find something
   b. the center of things
   c. to set aside
   d. to move out of place

3. **Dislocate**
   a. to move out of place
   b. the center
   c. to insult someone
   d. to give out or distribute

4. **Relocate**
   a. the center of activity
   b. to move to another place
   c. to move out of place
   d. to find someone

Make a sentence with each of the following words:

Relocate   Dislocate   Allocate   Locate

Challenge Words, look up these words in the dictionary:

Local   Localize   Locomotion

He: *Here, this looks like a perfect **location** for a picnic.*
She: *Of course, 50 million ants can't be wrong.*

VEN and VENT

The Latin roots **ven** and **vent** mean **to come**.

Venture: daring mission, risky business
Joel's <u>venture</u> was to take candies from home and sell them at school.
Joel's <u>risky business</u> deal was to take candies from home and sell them at school.

Adventure: a dangerous and exciting journey
Hansel and Gretel had many <u>adventures</u> as they tried to find their way home.
Hansel and Gretel had many <u>dangerous and exciting journeys</u> as they tried to find their way home.

Prevent: come before to stop something, to keep from happening
Wearing gloves during yard work will <u>prevent</u> injuries to hands.
Wearing gloves during yard work will <u>keep</u> hands from injury.

Convene: bring together, assemble
Alice decided to <u>convene</u> her softball team to figure out how to raise money.
Alice decided to <u>bring together</u> her softball team to figure out how to raise money.

Intervene: to come between
Mr. Pace had to <u>intervene</u> and stop the fight between the boys.
Mr. Pace had to <u>come between</u> the boys to stop them from fighting.

Tidbit

One of the great **adventures** of the century was Robert Perry and Matthew Henson's 1909 trip to the North Pole. They were the very first people to get there, but they had to endure freezing temperatures, sudden storms, and the risk of slow starvation. Even worse were cracks in the ice (called leads) that opened up to ocean water so cold that if you fell into it, you could drown or freeze to death in a single minute! Their **adventurous** spirit and bravery inspired others and the South Pole was discovered shortly afterwards.

Fill in each sentence with the correct word:

Venture   Adventure   Prevent   Convene   Intervene

1. Arnold knew that to _____ into the forest after the missing Frisbee was dangerous, so he decided to _____ a group of his friends and go in together.

2. Sandy and Andrea began fighting over who was going to hold the compass, until Arnold decided to _____ and make them hold it together. As they walked slowly into the dark and dense woods, they knew they were going to have a(n) _____.

3. If you wash your hands often during the day, you can _____ catching a cold or flu.

Choose the correct definition:

1. **Venture**
   a. to come together
   b. to interfere
   c. a risky business deal
   d. acting as a go-between

2. **Adventure**
   a. a risky business deal
   b. to interfere
   c. to come together
   d. a dangerous journey

3. **Convene**
   a. to come together
   b. an exciting journey
   c. to accuse of crime
   d. a risky business deal

4. **Intervene**
   a. an exciting journey
   b. to come between
   c. risky business
   d. to come together

Make a sentence with each of the following words:

Venture   Prevent   Convene   Intervene

Challenge Words, look up these words in the dictionary:

Convention   Venue

*A passerby **intervenes** in a fight between two boys: Shame on you, friends should not fight.*
The boys: *We are not friends, we are brothers!*

OID

This suffix means **like** or **resembling**.

Spheroid: shaped like a sphere or ball, but not perfectly round
Even though the Earth looks like a perfect marble from space, it is actually a spheroid.
Even though the Earth looks like a perfect marble from space, it is actually only shaped like a sphere but not perfectly round.

Meteoroid: a rock-like object from outer space that hits the earth
In astronomy class we learned that a meteoroid can look like a star with a tail.
In astronomy class we learned that rocks from outer space can look like a star with a tail.

Factoid: a small piece of information or fact which may or may not be true
Whenever you speak to Jeremy, he always starts with a random factoid to impress you.
Whenever you speak to Jeremy, he always starts with a random piece of information to impress you.

Humanoid: looking like a human in shape and appearance
Many outer space villains in cartoons look like humanoid.
Many outer space villains in cartoons look like humans.

Tidbit

 Random **factoids** get tossed around in conversation all the time. Whether they're true or not is another matter, but here are some that are. Dentists recommend that a toothbrush be kept at least 6 feet away from toilets to avoid airborne germs that come from flushing. Earthquakes are not rare at all - several hundred earthquakes occur every day. They occur even on the moon. Also, did you know you burn more calories sleeping than you do watching television? Finally, Walt Disney was afraid of mice, even though he created Mickey Mouse!

Fill in each sentence with the correct word:

Factoid   Meteoroid   Humanoid   Spheroid

1. Even though they aren't human, many apes are definitely _____ in appearance.

2. A _____ is often formed when bits of large comets break off and fall down to earth.

3. The snowman's head was _____ but looked almost perfectly round.

4. A fun _____ is that your hair grows faster at night.

Choose the correct definition:

1. **Spheroid**
   a. square
   b. resembling a sphere
   c. a random fact
   d. looking like a person

2. **Meteoroid**
   a. a comet
   b. a meteorite
   c. a solid object traveling through space
   d. resembling a sphere

3. **Factoid**
   a. a random interesting information
   b. resembling a person
   c. a solid object
   d. looking circular

4. **Humanoid**
   a. resembling a person
   b. looking round
   c. a random fact
   d. resembling my cat

Make a sentence with each of the following words:

Spheroid   Meteoroid   Factoid   Humanoid

Challenge Words, look up these words in the dictionary:

Asteroid   Ovoid (hint: ovo means egg)

In Astronomy class.
Teacher: Can anyone name a star with a tail?
Tommy: Micky Mouse!

EX

The Latin prefix **ex** means **out** or **previous**.

Exhale: to breathe out
Whenever Jen gets on a roller coaster, she holds her breath and forgets to <u>exhale</u>.
Whenever Jen gets on a roller coaster, she holds her breath and forgets to <u>breathe out</u>.

Exceed: to go beyond limits
Tammy knew her piano solo would <u>exceed</u> her parent's expectations because she had been secretly practicing for months.
Tammy knew her piano solo would <u>go beyond</u> her parent's expectations because she had been secretly practicing for months.

Ex-governor: the old or former governor
After leaving the office, the **ex-**<u>governor</u> decided to teach at the university.

Exhausted: totally out of energy; worn out, something that's all used up
Kelly was totally <u>exhausted</u> while only half way up the mountain.
Kelly was totally <u>worn out</u> while only half way up the mountain.

Here are some more words that begin with the prefix **ex**:
Expand: to spread out
Excess: to go out of limits, do more than others do
Extend: to make longer; stretch out, give more time

Confusion Alert!

The word **except** sounds very much like **accept,** which means to receive, approve, or include. The two words share the same root but have opposite meaning because of their different prefixes.

Tidbit

 A *little* bit of **excess** is usually okay once in a while. Who hasn't tried to eat an entire foot-tall hot fudge sundae by themselves, or at least wanted to? But some people take it to the **extreme**. One such man is Richard LeFevre, who set a world record by eating 6 pounds of Spam in 12 minutes. Another champion, Joey Chestnut, ate 103 hamburgers in 8 minutes. Sonya Thomas, who weighed only 105 pounds, ate 38 lobsters in 12 minutes.

Fill in each sentence with the correct word:

Exhausted   Ex-governor   Exceed   Exhale

1. Evelyn managed to _____ her own record to win the game, but afterwards she was so _____ that she could barely walk.

2. After he'd eaten 3 slices of garlic bread, Mark tried not to _____ into anyone's face.

3. Jesse Ventura, the _____ of Minnesota, is also an ex-wrestler.

Choose the correct definition:

1. **Exhale**
   a. the old governor
   b. to breathe out
   c. to breathe in
   d. to be tired

2. **Exceed**
   a. to breathe out
   b. out of energy
   c. to go beyond limits
   d. a former seed

3. **Ex-governor**
   a. the former governor
   b. out of energy
   c. the former mayor
   d. a former piece of fruit

4. **Exhausted**
   a. breathing out
   b. what cars make
   c. to go beyond limits
   d. totally out of energy, worn out

Make a sentence with each of the following words:

Exhausted   Excess   Exceed   Exhale

Challenge Words, look up these words in the dictionary:

Excavator   Exaggerate   Extinct

Boy: *Mom, I saw a dog as big as a horse!*
Mom: *I told you one hundred million times, never,* **exaggerate**.

TRACT

The Latin root **tract-** means to **draw** or **pull**.

Tractor: machine that pulls or digs
Our neighbor Duane helped us move the fallen tree with his <u>tractor</u>.
Our neighbor Duane helped us move the fallen tree with a <u>machine that pulls</u>.

Attract: to draw toward, catch the attention of
Fishermen use bait to <u>attract</u> the fish towards the lure.
Fishermen use bait to <u>draw</u> the fish towards the lure.

Contract: an agreement between two or more people
My sister and I have a <u>contract</u> that we don't tattle on each other.
My sister and I have an <u>agreement</u> that we don't tattle on each other.

Extract: to take out, draw out, pull out, or remove
Ryan worried that the dentist would have to <u>extract</u> his tooth.
Ryan worried that the dentist would have to <u>pull out</u> his tooth.

Retract: to take back, to pull back
After trying the snails again, Adam <u>retracted</u> his statement that they tasted bad.
After trying the snails again, Adam <u>took back</u> his statement that they tasted bad.

Intractable: unable to discipline; stubborn; difficult to treat (if a disease)
Every night she went to bed with an <u>intractable</u> headache.
Every night she went to bed with a <u>stubborn, difficult to treat</u> headache.

Tidbit

There are a lot of differences between cats and dogs, but a big one is **retractable** claws. Cats have a protective sheath of skin that keeps their claws sharp and hidden. But when they stretch or pounce, the claws come out of the sheath and can dig into things. Dogs don't have **retractable** claws, which means that their claws get worn down because they're always out. Because of their dull claws, dogs can only use their teeth as weapons. This is also a reason that dogs form packs to hunt and cats, the big ones, often hunt alone.

Fill in each sentence with the correct word:

Attract   Contract   Extract   Retract

1. Megan tried to _____ the kitten by offering it food. Finally, the kitten decided to _____ its claws, and let Megan scratch it behind the ears.

2. Paul's plan was to make a _____ with the teacher that if he stays awake in class, she won't give him a lot of homework.

3. Anthony fell in the manhole and they had to _____ him out of it with ropes and harness.

Choose the correct definition:

1. **Attract**
   a. a kind of rat
   b. to divert
   c. to draw towards
   d. an agreement

2. **Contract**
   a. to draw away
   b. an agreement
   c. to remove
   d. to take back

3. **Intractable**
   a. stubborn
   b. to pull out
   c. a draw toward
   d. to take back

4. **Retract**
   a. to push toward
   b. to turn away
   c. a kitten
   d. to pull back

Make a sentence with each of the following words:

Retract   Extract   Contract   Attract

Challenge Words, look up these words in the dictionary:

Protracted (hint: prefix pro means forward)
Detract (hint: prefix de means away)

> An excited boy runs into the house.
> **Dad**: What's the good news, son?
> **Boy**: They extended my **contract** for the third grade for one more year!

VOC and VOK

These roots mean **voice** or **call**.

Vocabulary: a collection of words, the number of words a person knows
O. Henry had a large <u>vocabulary</u> which helped him to become a great writer.
O. Henry knew a <u>lot of words</u> which helped him to become a great writer.

Provoke: to make one angry; to call forth emotions, usually anger but can be laughter
It is best not to <u>provoke</u> your opponent by teasing him.
It is best not to <u>make angry</u> your opponent by teasing him.

Vocal: relating to the voice; speaking openly and freely
The young choir member was <u>vocal</u> about her <u>vocal</u> talent.
The young choir member <u>spoke open and freely</u> about the beauty of her <u>voice</u>.

Vocation: a call to serve in a particular line of work, a profession
From a young age, Sally knew her <u>vocation</u> would be teaching.
From a young age, Sally felt a call to serve in <u>the field of</u> teaching.

Confusion Alert!

Don't confuse **vocation** with **vacation**. While a **vocation** refers to someone's line of work, a **vacation** is what you do when you *don't* work!

Tidbit

The larynx, commonly known as the voice box, is a tubular chamber about two inches high with **vocal** cords inside, that we use to make sounds. During silent breathing, the **vocal** cords rest along the larynx walls, leaving the air passage fully open. During speech, the cords stretch across the larynx. Air released from the lungs is forced between the cords, causing them to vibrate and produce sound. Since men's larynxes are usually larger than women's, male **vocal** cords tend to be longer, which is why their voices are deeper.

Fill in each sentence with the correct word:

Vocabulary   Provoke   Vocal   Vocation

1. Rachel had a large _____, her parents hoped that she would seek her _____ in the field of journalism.
2. Though Mark thought he was whispering quietly, the teacher told him to stop being so _____ in class.
3. Some students might have tried to _____ the teacher by talking back, but Mark stopped whispering right away.

Choose the correct definition:

1. **Provoke**
   a. to call forth anger
   b. a collection of words
   c. in favor of driving
   d. audible or oral

2. **Vocabulary**
   a. to call forth anger
   b. a collection of words
   c. audible or oral
   d. quiet

3. **Vocation**
   a. a holiday
   b. a collection of words and phrases
   c. a call to serve in a certain job
   d. audible or oral

4. **Vocal**
   a. to call forth anger
   b. to express in voice
   c. audible or oral
   d. quiet

Make a sentence with each of the following words:

Vocal   Vocation   Provoke

Challenge Words, look up these words in the dictionary:

Invoke   Revoke   Vociferous

In a pet store.
The customer: *This talking parrot, does it have a large* **vocabulary**?
The store owner: *You know, he was asking the same question about you.*

DEM

The Greek root **dem** means **people**.

Democracy: government formed by the people and for the people
The American form of government is called a democracy.
The American form of government is called a government by the people and for the people.

Endemic: specific or common in a particular area, often a disease
Malaria, a sickness caused by mosquitoes, is endemic in Africa.
Malaria, a sickness caused by mosquitoes, is widespread and common in Africa.

Epidemic: a sickness that spreads quickly and affects many people
There was a flu epidemic at school, so half the students and teachers were out sick.
There was a widespread sickness at school, so half the students and teachers were out sick.

Demagogue: a leader of a mob who excites people through lies
Some people still think that Mussolini was a great leader, but the others believe he was a dangerous demagogue.
Some people still think that Mussolini was a great leader, but the others believe he was a dangerous mob leader.

Demography: a study of people, age, income, places, etc.
Professor Morgan is interested in the demography of the African countries.
Professor Morgan is interested in a study of people of the African countries.

Tidbit

The word **democracy** comes from the Greek word *demos*, meaning "people," and *kratos*, meaning "rule." Even though the Ancient Greeks invented **democracy**, they did not let everyone take part in it. The only people that could vote and have a say in their government were adult Greek men, which only made up 25% of the population. Women, children, slaves, and anybody not born in Greece could not vote. Maybe they were not as democratic as we think.

Fill in each sentence with the correct word:

Democracy   Endemic   Epidemic   Demagogue

1. As Bobby studied Ethiopia, he found out that hunger was _____ throughout the nation.

2. The school principal knew that letting everyone vote in the school election would be a great lesson in _____.

3. When Jason promised to get rid of homework if elected school president, I knew he was simply a power-hungry _____ .

4. In 2001, an_____ of hoof-and-mouth disease made cattle sick all over Britain.

Choose the correct definition:

1. **Democracy**
   a. government by the people
   b. a Greek city
   c. a political party
   d. widespread and common

2. **Demagogue**
   a. a Greek philosopher
   b. any politician who tells lies
   c. a sport announcer
   d. a government ruled by the people

3. **Endemic**
   a. specific for a place
   b. finals
   c. a kind of government
   d. a member of the Democratic Party

4. **Epidemic**
   a. a member of a political party
   b. a kind of government
   c. a type of a headache
   d. an illness that moves quickly and wide

Make a sentence with each of the following words:

Democracy   Endemic   Epidemic   Demography

One cow to the other: *Did you hear about the **epidemic** of mad cow disease?*
The other cow: *What do I care, I am a helicopter!*

POP

The Latin root **pop** means **people**.

Popular: well-known, having many friends
Ted was the most popular kid at school because he made friends with everyone.
Ted was well-known by the kids at school because he made friends with everyone.

Population: the number of people in a certain place
The town was so small that it only had a population of 300 people.
The town was so small that only 300 people lived there.

Populate: to fill with people, to live in, inhabit
The silkworms reproduced to populate the shoebox that was their home.
The silkworms reproduced to fill-up the shoebox that was their home.

Populous: full of people
New York City is the most populous American city with more than eight million people.
New York City is the most people-filled American city with more than eight million people.

Confusion Alert!

Populous looks and sounds like **populace**, which is another word for "the people." For example, if everyone in town voted for a new mayor, you might say, "The town's populace voted for a new mayor."

Tidbit

 According to the most recent publications, the world **population** hit 6.5 billion in 2006. It is projected that by 2012, the Earth will be home to 7 billion people. China is the world's most **populous** country, with a **population** of over a billion people - about 1/6 of the entire world's **population**! The United States, on the other hand, has about 300 million people, which means China's **population** is more than 4 times bigger than ours. India is the second largest country with over a billion people. The world's *least* **populous** country is Vatican City with an official **population** of 281.

Fill in each sentence with the correct word:

Popular   Population   Populate   Populous

1. Baseball caps are so _____ that it seems the entire _____ of America wears them.

2. The very _____ town barely had enough houses for everyone.

3. Usually the people that _____ cities by the ocean love nature, swimming, and sailing.

Choose the correct definition:

1. **Popular**
   a. filled with people
   b. the total number of people
   c. baseball caps
   d. known by a lot of people

2. **Population**
   a. the number of people in a place
   b. accepted and known to others
   c. the New Yorkers
   d. to fill with people

3. **Populate**
   a. accepted and known by many
   b. to fill with people or live in
   c. the people of China
   d. full of people

4. **Populous**
   a. full of people
   b. a famous Greek politician
   c. accepted and known
   d. the number of people in a place

Make a sentence with each of the following words:

Popular   Population   Populate   Populous

Challenge Words, look up these words in the dictionary:

Popularize   Unpopular

Johnny: *Mom, dad, you have been invited to a very* **unpopular** *back-to-school night.*
Parents: *Why unpopular?*
Johnny: *Because the principal only wants to see you.*

DORM or HYPNO

The Latin root **dorm-** and the Greek root **hypno** both mean to **sleep**.

Dormitory: a dorm, a building where students sleep
Monica's <u>dormitory</u> roommate became her best friend.
Monica's <u>student housing</u> roommate became her best friend.

Dormant: sleeping, in a sleepy state, inactive
After dropping their leaves in fall, many trees remain <u>dormant</u> from November until March.
After dropping their leaves in fall, many trees remain <u>in a sleepy state</u> from November until March.

Dormer: a window that sticks out from a sloping roof, usually over a bedroom

Hypnotic: a medication that helps one fall asleep, putting someone in a trance
Mrs. Lerner's lectures are like a <u>hypnotic</u>, there isn't anyone awake in the entire class.
Mrs. Lerner's lectures are like <u>sleeping pills</u>, there isn't anyone awake in the entire class.

Hypnotist: A trained specialist able to create a sleeplike state in someone
My uncle stopped snoring at night with the help of a <u>hypnotist.</u>
My uncle stopped snoring at night with the help of a <u>trained specialist who was able to put him in a trance.</u>

Tidbit

Hypnosis, from Greek root **hypno**, describes a state in which someone is half awake and half asleep. When in a state of **hypnosis**, a person becomes relaxed and more open to suggestion. Sometimes **hypnosis** is used to treat certain problems, such as nervousness or phobias. Although probably known to the ancient Egyptians, **hypnosis** became popular in 18th century Europe, thanks to German doctor *Franz Anton Mesmer*. The verb mesmerize is used instead of **hypnotize** to honor Dr. Mesmer's work.

Fill in each sentence with the correct word:

Dormitory   Dormant   Hypnotic   Hypnosis

1. Victor's parents tried everything, even _____, to make him remember to brush his hair in the morning.

2. The music had a _____ effect and almost everyone in the concert hall fell asleep.

3. The _____ was almost empty, but Mr. Morpheus ran into several _____ students lying on their beds.

Choose the correct definition:

1. **Dormitory**
   a. sleepy state
   b. empty state
   c. a type of camel
   d. a place where students sleep

2. **Dormant**
   a. a mouse
   b. a mat in front of a door
   c. sleepy
   d. a place where students sleep

3. **Hypnotic**
   a. a sleepy state
   b. a medication to wake up
   c. a medication to treat a flu
   d. a magician

4. **Hypnosis**
   a. a type of music
   b. a magician
   c. a sleep-like state
   d. a famous Greek poet

Make a sentence with each of the following words:

Dormitory   Dormant   Hypnotic   Hypnosis

Customer: I can't sleep and need a **hypnotic**.
Pharmacist: Would you like an expensive or cheap one?
Customer: Cheap, of course.
Pharmacist: Very well. Rock-a-bye baby, in the treetops...

FLEX and FLECT

The Latin roots **flex-** and **flect-** mean **to bend.**

Flexible: bendable; changeable or adaptable
Micah was so <u>flexible</u> that she could put both her feet behind her head.
Micah was so <u>bendable</u> that she could put both her feet behind her head.

Inflection: the change of tone, character, or rise and fall of a voice
Even though he couldn't see her face, Ron could tell that Tina was upset by the <u>inflection</u> of her voice.
Even though he couldn't see her face, Ron could tell that Tina was upset by the <u>change of tone</u> in her voice.

Deflect: to bend away from, repel, turn aside
As they practiced karate, Sean managed to <u>deflect</u> most of Lindsay's kicks.
As they practiced karate, Sean managed to <u>turn aside</u> most of Lindsay's kicks.

Reflect: to return a mirror image; being thoughtful, to think seriously
In the prologue to his autobiography, the author <u>reflected</u> on his childhood in Georgia.
In the prologue to his autobiography, the author <u>thought seriously</u> about his childhood in Georgia.

Reflection: a mirror image; something that bounces back off another surface
Ashley stared silently at her <u>reflection</u> in the mirror after getting a new haircut.
Ashley stared silently at her <u>mirror image</u> after getting a new haircut.

Tidbit

Some people are so **flexible** that they can move and bend in ways that most people can't. These very bendy people are called contortionist. They are split up into two groups, depending on which way their spines bend: front-benders and back-benders. Some contortionist can tie themselves in knots, bend their backs so that their heads touch their feet, or fit into tiny boxes. If you have ever seen a contortionist, you might have wondered how they do it. Well, it's a combination of **flexible** joints and hard work. With enough training, almost anybody can learn some contortionist skills.

Fill in each sentence with the correct word:

Flexible   Inflection   Deflect   Reflection

1. Sandy noticed a fly buzzing toward her and managed to _____ it before it sat on her sandwich.

2. Hannah could tell by the _____ of Sam's voice that something had happened, but he refused to tell her what it was over the phone.

3. Luckily, Hannah's _____ schedule that day allowed her take time to go to Sam's house and insist that he tell her all.

4. The Loch Ness Monster looked at its own _____ in the lake's water and liked what it saw.

Choose the correct definition:

1. **Flexible**
   a. to bend aside
   b. bendable, changeable
   c. thoughtful
   d. a circus animal

2. **Inflection**
   a. the tone of a voice
   b. a disease from germs
   c. to bend away, repel
   d. thoughtful

3. **Deflect**
   a. bend backwards
   b. run away from the army
   c. tone of voice
   d. to turn aside, repel

4. **Reflective**
   a. thoughtful
   b. bendable
   c. to bend aside, repel
   d. tone of voice

Make a sentence with each of the following words:

Flexible   Inflection   Deflect   Reflective

Challenge Words, look up these words in the dictionary:

Genuflection (hint: genu means knees)   Inflexible   Reflex

At an Art Gallery.
A Visitor: *I suppose this horrible looking thing is what you call Modern Art?*
Art dealer: *I beg your pardon, Sir. That's your* **reflection** *in the mirror!*

FAC and FACT

The Latin roots **fac** and **fact** mean **to do** or **make**.

Factory: a place where things are made
We visited the candy <u>factory</u> and got free jellybeans.
We visited the <u>place where</u> candies <u>are made</u> and got free jellybeans.

Faculty: the ability to do something, a talent **OR** a group of teachers
The school's <u>faculty</u> had a great <u>faculty</u> for helping students to learn.
The school's <u>teachers</u> had a great <u>talent</u> for helping students to learn.

Factor: a part, one part out of many that make a whole, something that adds to a result
Being happy is a big <u>factor</u> in living a long life.
Being happy <u>plays a</u> big <u>part</u> in living a long life.

Artifact: a human-made object; an inaccurate observation
On the X-ray, it looked like the bone was broken, but Dr, said it was only an <u>artifact.</u>
On the X-ray, it looked like the bone was broken, but Dr, said it was an <u>inaccurate observation.</u>

Tidbit

 A **facsimile** is an exact copy of something else. A fax machine, which is short for **facsimile** machine, make perfect copies of documents or pictures that can be sent to others using a phone line. A Scottish mechanic named Alexander Bain invented the first fax machine in 1842. Over the next hundred years, other inventors improved the fax machine, and today, fax machines are used to send perfect copies of documents across the world instantly.

Fill in each sentence with the correct word:

Artifacts   Faculty   Factory   Factor

1. The hundreds of workers left the _____ at the end of the day.

2. Jim had a _____ for painting and won many prizes for his artwork.

3. Surprise is the biggest _____ in winning at dodge ball.

4. Many _____ can be found along the western trail left by the immigrants.

Choose the correct definition:

1. **Artifact**
   a. an exact copy
   b. human-made object
   c. a place where things are made
   d. jelly beans

2. **Factor**
   a. a truck on a farm
   b. a teacher
   c. something that adds to a result
   d. an inaccurate observation

3. **Artifact**
   a. a fax machine
   b. made up, not real
   c. a man-made object
   d. something that adds to a result

4. **Faculty**
   a. a talent or a group of teachers
   b. an exact copy
   c. a school dance
   d. a place where things are made

Make a sentence with each of the following words:

Artifact   Artifact   Factor   Faculty

Challenge Words, look up these words in the dictionary:

Facilitate   Facility

Q: *What's the difference between school* **faculty** *and a train engineer?*
A: *The* **faculty** *trains minds but the engineer minds the trains.*

FLU

The root **flu-** means **flowing**.

Fluid: a flowing substance, a liquid
After Ross broke his jaw, he drank only <u>fluids</u> because he couldn't chew.
After Ross broke his jaw, he drank only <u>liquids</u> because he couldn't chew.

Fluctuate: to change unsteadily, shift or swing from one thing to another
It seems that babies can <u>fluctuate</u> between happy and sad a dozen times within a matter of minutes.
It seems that babies' moods can <u>swing</u> between happy and sad a dozen times within a matter of minutes.

Influence: to sway or affect something, to convince, to control
Joel always tried to <u>influence</u> his brother by setting a good example.
Joel always tried to <u>convince</u> his brother by setting a good example.

Affluent: rich, wealthy
For her birthday, Jenny wants a new coat from her <u>affluent</u> uncle and aunt.
For her birthday, Jenny wants a new coat from her <u>rich</u> uncle and aunt.

Flute: a musical instrument

Confusion Alert!
There are two words that sound very similar and share the same root **flu**. The first word is **flue** - a pipe through which smoke can escape from a chimney. The other word is **flu**, about which you can read below.

Tidbit

Almost everyone has caught the **flu** at some point in their life. It's miserable having the flu, but at least the origin of its name is neat. The word **flu** is short for the word **influenza**, a word that comes from the Latin word *influencia*. *Influencia* was thought to be a fluid given off by certain stars that ruled the human world. *Influencia* eventually became the Italian word *influenza*, which was any kind of plague or sickness blamed on the stars. Influenza became known as the cold-like sickness that we know today as "the **flu**" during a very bad outbreak in 1743 Italy.

Fill in each sentence with the correct word:

Fluid   Fluctuate   Influence   Affluent

1. The dancers in the video all moved in one _____ motion.

2. The announcer said that the temperature during the week would _____ from 10° to 50°.

3. Allen tried to _____ his parents to buy the big-screen TV, but was told that they weren't _____ enough to afford it.

Choose the correct definition:

1. **Fluid**
   a. to sway or move something
   b. rich, wealthy
   c. a liquid
   d. a musical instrument

2. **Fluctuate**
   a. to become rich
   b. to shift from one thing to another
   c. a flowing substance
   d. a kind of virus

3. **Influence**
   a. a liquid
   b. a disease
   c. an arriving airplane
   d. to persuade

4. **Affluent**
   a. rich, wealthy
   b. an illness
   c. a liquid
   d. to waver

Make a sentence with each of the following words:

Fluid   Fluctuate   Influence   Affluent

Challenge Words, look up these words in the dictionary:

Fluent   Superfluous

Teacher: Why did you miss school yesterday?
Tony: My brother had the **flu**.
Teacher: So?
Tony: I rode his scooter all day.

LIC and LICIT

The Latin roots **lic-** and **licit** mean **permit** or **allow**.

License: a permit, freedom to act
Sarah planned to get her driver's <u>license</u> the minute she turned 16.
Sarah planned to get her <u>permit</u> to drive the minute she turned 16.

> Other licenses are
> **Marriage license**: permission to get married
> **Medical license**: permission to practice medicine
> **Fishing license**: permission to fish

Solicit: to ask or beg for something
Mark tried to <u>solicit</u> his mom's help in baking the cake, but ended up making it himself.
Mark tried to <u>ask</u> his mom's help in baking the cake, but ended up making it himself.

Explicit: clear, plain, well-defined
Amy's instructions were <u>explicit</u> – no one was to talk during the test!
Amy's instructions were <u>clear</u> – no one was to talk during the test!

Illicit: against the law, unlawful, illegal
The police shut down the <u>illicit</u> gambling club.
The police shut down the <u>unlawful</u> gambling club.

Confusion Alert!

Illicit is similar to the word **elicit**, but they have very different meanings. **Elicit** means **to draw out**. For example, you might try to elicit feelings in others by reading a poem.

Tidbit

The police enforce all the laws, **licenses**, and permits that our country has. Sometimes they get into pretty funny situations. In South Dakota, police spotted a car driving recklessly (wildly) at 90 miles an hour in a 55 mile an hour zone. Three police cars went after it, but the car wouldn't slow down. The car finally pulled into an animal clinic parking lot and a man ran out with a goose. His dog had bitten the goose, so he thought he needed to get it to the veterinarian as soon as possible, so he drove as fast as he could, even with the police behind him. The moral of the story is: don't lead the police on a wild goose chase even if you actually have a goose!

Big Words for Little Kids

Fill in each sentence with the correct word:

Illicit   Solicit   License   Explicit

1. Janet went door to door to _____ her neighbors for charity donations.

2. Albert couldn't wait to get his driver's _____ so he thought about getting a fake one by _____ means.

3. Greg gave _____ directions to his house, but we got lost anyway.

Choose the correct definition:

1. **Illicit**
   a. sick
   b. against the law
   c. to beg
   d. a permit

2. **License**
   a. to ask
   b. unlawful
   c. a permit
   d. a secret agent

3. **Explicit**
   a. clear and plain
   b. unlawful
   c. a permit
   d. authorized

4. **Solicit**
   a. lawful
   b. unlawful
   c. authorized
   d. to ask or beg

Make a sentence with each of the following words:

License   Illicit   Explicit   Solicit

Challenge Words, look up these words in the dictionary:

Unlicensed   Licensing

*A teacher asks a student to **solicit** his neighbors for raffle tickets. The boy comes back in 15 minutes and says he sold all his tickets.*
Teacher: *How did you do it?*
Student: *I am not sure, but at the first house they bought all the tickets after their dog bit me.*

MIGRA

The Latin root **migra** means to **wander.**

Migrate: travel, move from place to place
Geese <u>migrate</u> to warmer places every winter.
Geese <u>travel</u> to warmer places every winter.

Immigrate: move to a new land to live
Max's family <u>immigrated</u> to America after his father lost his job in Italy.
Max's family <u>moved to</u> America after his father lost his job in Italy.

Immigrant: a person that goes to live in a new land
Christina's dad was an <u>immigrant</u> who came to America from Korea when he was six.
Christina's dad <u>moved to</u> America from Korea when he was six.

Emigrate: leave a country and live in another
Peter decided to <u>emigrate from</u> Russia to start over in another country.
Peter decided to <u>leave</u> Russia to start over in another country.

Confusion Alert!

<u>I</u>mmigrate and <u>e</u>migrate sound alike but mean opposite things. Immigrate means to COME TO a country, while emigrate means to LEAVE FROM a country. So, Mr. Chan would EMIGRATE **from** China, and IMMIGRATE **to** America.

Tidbit

 Migration means movement of people or animals from one place to another. One of North America's most amazing natural events is the great annual **migration** of the beautiful monarch butterfly. Every year, nearly 300 million of these beautiful butterflies **Migrate** from Canada and the northeastern United States in order to take a 2,500-mile journey to Mexico in the fall, only for next generation to fly back to Canada in the spring.

Fill in each sentence with the correct word:

Migrate   Immigrant   Immigrate   Emigrate

1. Paula wanted to live in another country, so she decided to _____
   from Poland. Even though she missed her old home, she was glad that she
   decided to _____ to America.

2. Lisa's family would _____ from place to place, never living in one
   town for more than a few years.

3. Since Pablo was a new _____, he had trouble speaking English.

Choose the correct definition:

1. **Migrate**
   a. a person that comes to a new land   c. to move from place to place
   b. migration   d. to leave a place to live in a new one

2. **Immigrant**
   a. a monarch butterfly   c. to wander from place to place
   b. one who comes to a new land   d. one who leaves the old land

3. **Immigrate**
   a. to wander from place to place   c. a person that has no place to stay
   b. to go from a country   d. to move to a new country to live

4. **Emigrate**
   a. to leave from one country   c. to wander from place to place
   b. one who comes to a new land   d. cutting cheese

Make a sentence with each of the following words:

Migrate   Immigrant   Immigrate   Emigrate

Challenge Words, look up these words in the dictionary:

Migrant   Migratory

Teacher: *Which birds do not **migrate**?*
Student: *Cuckoo birds.*
Teacher: *Why?*
Student: *They live inside clocks.*

MOB, MOT, and MOV

The roots **mob**, **mot**, and **mov** mean **move**.

Motion: movement
With a single swift <u>motion</u>, Amy chopped the board in half with her hand.
With a single swift <u>movement</u>, Amy chopped the board in half with her hand.

Motivation: the reason for an action, a push to act certain way
Amy's desire to get even with her older brother was her <u>motivation</u> for learning karate.
Amy's desire to get even with her older brother was her <u>reason</u> for learning karate.

Emotional: moved strongly by feelings
He felt <u>emotional</u> after his friend's family moved to another state.
He felt <u>strong feelings</u> about his friend moving to another state.

Promotion: move forward in rank; advertise to make a product popular
Demotion: lowering in rank or position, opposite of promotion
Gordon expected a <u>promotion</u> for his bright idea; instead, he received a <u>demotion</u> when they found out that the idea wasn't his.
Gordon expected to <u>move up in the company</u> because of his bright idea; instead, he was <u>moved down</u> when they found out that the idea wasn't his.

Immobile: not moving, motionless
Brent sat <u>immobile</u> in the bushes with his paintball gun, waiting for someone from the opposing team to wander by.
Brent sat <u>not moving</u> in the bushes with his paintball gun, waiting for someone from the opposing team to wander by.

Tidbit

A **mobile** is a toy-like object made of rods and strings that hang freely from above while balancing and spinning around. Modern **mobiles** were created in 1931 by an American sculptor named Alexander Calder, but it was the French artist Marcel Duchamp who suggested the name. The name **mobile** applies to any sculpture where motion is the most important feature. **Mobiles** are particularly common in nurseries because they give babies something fun and ever-changing to look at.

Fill in each sentence with the correct word:

Motivation   Emotional   Immobile   Motion

1. Kara always cries and feels _____ during sad movies.

2. John's _____ for practicing the guitar was his dream of becoming a rock star someday.

3. Baseball is a curious game. Most of the time, the players are _____, standing around and waiting. Then suddenly everybody is in _____ chasing the ball and running the bases.

Choose the correct definition:

1. **Immobile**
   a. capable of moving
   b. bouncing off the walls
   c. not moving
   d. moved by feelings

2. **Emotional**
   a. not moving
   b. capable of moving
   c. moved by feelings
   d. a mechanical power

3. **Motion**
   a. picture
   b. not moved by feelings
   c. moved by feelings
   d. movement

4. **Motivation**
   a. not moving
   b. reason for an action
   c. mechanical power
   d. movement

Make a sentence with each of the following words:

Mobile   Emotional   Motivation   Motion   Promotion

Challenge Words, look up these words in the dictionary:

Mobilization   Motorcade

Alex's new **mobile** phone rings.
Dad: Alex, how do you like your new phone?
Alex: I like it. But, dad, how did you know I am in the playground?

AUD

The Latin root **aud** means to **hear** or **listen**.

Audible: can be heard
John's whispering was barely <u>audible</u>.
John's whispering could barely be <u>heard</u>.

Inaudible: impossible to hear
Because of the noise, Martin's speech was <u>inaudible</u> to most guests.
Because of the noise, Martin's speech was <u>impossible to hear</u> by most guests.

Audience: a group of people gathered together to watch or listen to something; also a chance to be heard by an important person
The <u>audience</u> enjoyed the concert put on by the band.
The <u>people gathered to watch the show</u> enjoyed the concert put on by the band.

Audition: a hearing or tryout, usually for singers or actors
Half the school went to the <u>audition</u> to get on the television game show.
Half the school went to the <u>tryout</u> to get on the television game show.

Auditorium: a large room in a theater where the viewers or listeners sit
The parents were invited to the <u>auditorium</u> to watch the school show.
The parents were invited to the large room in the <u>theater</u> to watch the school show.

Tidbit

Audiologists study and test our hearing. The process of hearing is complex and uses many tiny "machines" in your ear. Sound enters the **auditory** canal and strikes your eardrum, causing it to vibrate. The sound continues to pass into the small opening leading to the middle ear. The small bones of the middle ear then vibrate, setting in motion the fluid of your inner ear. Changes in pressure move tiny hair cells, which send signal to special cells that then send signals along the **auditory** nerve to the brain. The brain receives these signals and translates them into recognizable words, sounds, and music.

Fill in each sentence with the correct word:

Audience   Audible   Auditorium   Audition

1. When little Matt finished his piano piece, the _____ cheered loudly.

2. Dan opened his eyes and nervously looked at the people in the _____.

3. The voice from the television was so low it was barely _____.

4. The singer got nervous and developed hiccups right before his _____.

Choose the correct definition:

1. **Audition**
   a. a hearing or tryout
   b. a group of listeners
   c. can be heard
   d. a person who listens

2. **Audience**
   a. a hearing or tryout
   b. a group of listeners
   c. something odd
   d. a car that rushes to an accident

3. **Audible**
   a. a hearing or tryout
   b. a foreign car
   c. can be heard
   d. cannot be heard

4. **Inaudible**
   a. loud and clear
   b. a person who listens
   c. can be heard
   d. can't be heard

Make a sentence with each of the following words:

Audience   Audible   Audition   Auditorium

Challenge Words, look up these words in the dictionary:

Auditor   Audiometer

The Singer: *I think I failed the **audition**.*
The Friend: *Why?*
The Singer: *The director woke up in the middle of my singing and cried: "Can someone let the poor dog in?"*

POTEN and POSSE

The Latin roots **poten** and **posse** mean **power**.

Potent: powerful, effective, strong
To cure Jonathan's cold, his mother made the most <u>potent</u> treatment – chicken soup.
To cure Jonathan's cold, his mother made the most <u>powerful</u> and <u>effective</u> treatment – chicken soup.

Potential: able to move forward; ability to grow, or improve
Joel has a lot of <u>potential</u>. He can become anything he wants when he grows up.
Joel has a lot of <u>ability</u>. He can become anything he wants when he grows up.

Possession: ownership of property, wealth, territory; a belonging
Every day, Mr. Porter went to check on his prized <u>possession</u> – his green tractor.
Every day, Mr. Porter went to check on his prized <u>belonging</u> – his green tractor.

Possessed: being preoccupied, crazy; being out of control
Tim was excited about the vacation, but I think he acted like he was <u>possessed</u>.
Tim said he was excited about the vacation, but I think he acted like he was <u>crazy</u>.

Tidbit

 Can you believe that when Albert Einstein was a child, his relatives thought he wasn't very smart? Little did they know of Einstein's incredible **potential** for genius. During the first four years of his life, little Albert could not speak at all. In his early school years, he spoke very slowly and took a long time to think about what he was going to say. At first, his parents feared that there was something wrong with him. He didn't do very well in many of his subjects, though he always showed great **potential** in math. When Einstein was five, his father showed him a pocket compass. Seeing a compass needle moving left a lasting impression on him. As a result, Einstein wrote his first scientific work on magnetism at the age of fifteen. Eventually, he grew into one of the most famous scientist of all time!

Fill in each sentence with the correct word:

Potent   Potential   Possessions   Possessed

1. Chris made a _____ argument in favor of skipping lunch so they could spend their money on video games.

2. My father always said, "We don't want too many _____, it keeps you tied down."

3. The moment the ball hit Annie's bat, everyone knew it had the _____ to be a homerun. When it did, all in the stadium jumped as if they were _____.

Choose the correct definition:

1. **Potent**
   a. powerful, strong, effective   c. to own
   b. a kind of pot   d. possible

2. **Potential**
   a. all-powerful   c. to own
   b. having the possibility of growth   d. strong, effective

3. **Possession**
   a. having the possibility of growth   c. ownership
   b. a moving crowd   d. all-powerful

4. **Possessed**
   a. acting crazy   c. all-powerful
   b. strong, effective   d. a possibility

Make a sentence with each of the following words:

Potent   Potential   Possession   Possessed

Challenge Words, look up these words in the dictionary:

Potency   Possible   Impossible

Student: *Is it **possible** that you will punish me for something I didn't do?*
Teacher: *Of course not.*
Student: *I didn't do my homework.*

OB and OP

The Latin prefixes **ob-** and **op-** mean **in the way** and **against**.

Obstruct: to be in the way, to block
Colin's seat at the concert had a huge column in front that <u>obstructed</u> his view.
Colin's seat at the concert had a huge column in front that <u>blocked</u> his view.

Oppose: to set against, to resist
The Governor <u>opposed</u> every attempt to change the helmet law.
The Governor <u>resisted</u> every attempt to change the helmet law.

Oppress: keep down, control, bully
The kingdom <u>oppressed</u> its people until the revolution finally changed it all.
The kingdom <u>kept control of</u> its people until the revolution finally changed it all.

Obscure: hard to see, unclear, hidden, confusing, hard to understand
As she was hiking up the hill, Jenny hoped the fog would not <u>obscure</u> the beautiful view.
As she was hiking up the hill, Jenny hoped the fog would not <u>hide</u> the beautiful view.

Obstinate: being stubborn, unmoving, pigheaded
Ashley's <u>obstinate</u> dog sat on top of her artwork and refused to move.
Ashley's <u>stubborn</u> dog sat on top of her artwork and refused to move.

Tidbit

To survive in this world, many plants and animals have to be strong and stubborn. Unfortunately, many of the most **obstinate** are the most annoying to humans. One of the world's worst weeds, a prickly shrub with pretty yellow flowers called gorse, is incredibly **obstinate** and refuses to die. Bulldozers, fire, and herbicide fail to kill it. Originally from England, it now covers huge chunks of Australia, Europe, and America. The plant can lie dormant for over 30 years, until some gardener disturbs the soil and the gorse starts shooting its seeds up to 30 feet from plant. Talk about **obstinate**!

Fill in each sentence with the correct word:

Obstruct   Oppress   Obscure   Obstinate

1. During the family picture session, Victor decided to be _____ and not smile.

2. From history, Sandra knew some people tried to _____ others because of the color of their skin, which she thought was pretty strange.

3. People couldn't recognize Tom at all on Halloween because of the mask he used to _____ his face.

4. Terry liked running early because there were no others runners to _____ his path.

Choose the correct definition:

1. **Obstruct**
   a. to be in the way, to block
   b. stubborn, unmoving
   c. hard to see
   d. to bully

2. **Oppress**
   a. to push hard
   b. getting grounded for a month
   c. keep down, dominate, bully
   d. to block

4. **Obscure**
   a. pigheaded
   b. hard to see, unclear, hidden
   c. a kind of weed
   d. bully, keep down

5. **Obstinate**
   a. stubborn, unmoving, inflexible
   b. to be in the way
   c. not voting
   d. hidden

Make a sentence with each of the following words:

Obstruct   Oppose   Oppress   Obscure   Obstinate

Challenge Words, look up these words in the dictionary:

Oblivious   Obtuse   Opponent   Object

> **Johnny** *asks the neighbor: Can you please give me a lift to my school?*
> **Neighbor:** *But I am traveling in* **opposite** *direction.*
> **Johnny:** *That's even better!*

NON

The prefix **non-** means **not.**

Nonbeliever: someone who does not believe, doubtful person
When it came to space aliens, Jared was a <u>nonbeliever</u> for sure.
When it came to space aliens, Jared was a <u>doubter</u> for sure.

Nonchalant: having an appearance of not caring, casual, cool, unconcerned
Derek was <u>nonchalant</u> when he heard about the accident. He just shrugged and said, "It happens."
Derek seemed <u>unconcerned</u> when he heard about the accident. He just shrugged and said, "It happens."

Nonconformist: a person who doesn't want to be like everyone else
Sharon thought she was a <u>nonconformist</u> because she dressed all in black.
Sharon thought she <u>wasn't like anyone else</u> because she dressed all in black.

Nondescript: unremarkable, plain, not interesting, or dull
The house looked <u>nondescript</u> from the outside, but the inside was bright and colorful.
The house looked <u>plain and dull</u> from the outside, but the inside was bright and colorful.

More words that use the prefix **non**:
Nonprofit: not planning to earn a lot of money
Nonsense: words that have bizarre meaning or no meaning at all
Nonstop: without stopping
You can make new words, called neologism (neo means new, logo is word) by putting prefix non- in front of it. For example: nonfriend, nontrue, noncooked, and noncute.

Tidbit

Many things on our planet that we use every day are **nonrenewable**. That means we can't restore them, or make more of them, once we've used them up. Some of these **nonrenewable** resources are oil and natural gas, which we use to run our cars and heat our homes. Another is metal ore, which we use to make everything metal from steel to gold and silver. Many of these natural resources are limited and may run out if we use them up too fast. That's why many people have started to recycle and use renewable energy like solar power which is unlimited.

Fill in each sentence with the correct word:

Nondescript   Nonconformist   Nonchalant   Nonbeliever

1. Jill always tried to be a _____ with her unusual clothes and behavior. Her sister Jenna, however, always wore _____ clothing so she wouldn't draw attention to herself.

2. Becky was a _____ in the Loch Ness Monster. She couldn't believe that there was a 50-foot dinosaur still alive and swimming in that lake.

3. Henry always pretended to be cool and _____, but on the inside he was always worrying what others think.

Choose the correct definition:

1. **Nonbeliever**
   a. cool, unconcerned
   b. a doubtful person
   c. wants to be different
   d. dull, uninteresting

2. **Nonchalant**
   a. can't be reused
   b. ordinary, dull
   c. cool, unconcerned
   d. not like others

3. **Nonconformist**
   a. a title of a movie
   b. uninteresting, ordinary
   c. unconcerned, indifferent
   d. doesn't want to be like others

4. **Nondescript**
   a. dull, ordinary
   b. wants to stand out
   c. doesn't believe in anything
   d. unconcerned, indifferent

Make a sentence with each of the following words:

Nondescript   Nonchalant   Nonbeliever   Nonrenewable

Challenge Words, look up these words in the dictionary:

Nonessential   Nonjudgmental

Customer: *Waiter, I think my chicken is **non-cooked**.*
Waiter: *What makes you say that?*
Customer: *It just ate my salad.*

DOM

The suffix -**dom** means **state** or **condition of**.

Wisdom: being wise, understanding, having good judgment
Max saw <u>wisdom</u> in his mom's decision to keep him inside during the snow storm.
Max saw <u>good judgment</u> in his mom's decision to keep him inside during the snow storm.

Boredom: being bored, dull
At the end of summer, many kids experience <u>boredom</u> and are ready for school to start again.
At the end of summer, many kids feel <u>bored</u> and are ready for school to start again.

Freedom: the state of being free
There's a great sense of <u>freedom</u> after the last day of the school year.
There's a great sense of <u>being free</u> after the last day of the school year.

Kingdom: a country led by a king or monarch
It seems that in every fable there is a <u>kingdom</u> with a prince or princess who ends up getting married.
It seems that in every fable there is a <u>country with a king</u> with a prince or princess who ends up getting married.

Tidbit

In a really boring class, you can expect to see more than a few yawns. But is it **boredom** that causes us to yawn, or something else? A lot of research has gone into this, and millions of dollars have been spent trying to figure out what makes us yawn. Most scientists agree that **boredom** doesn't cause yawning, and many believe that it's caused by a lack of oxygen. When we yawn, we take a deep breath that replenishes our air supply. Many other scientists don't like this theory, but can't really come up with anything better. One thing we definitely know is that yawning is contagious: even reading about yawning makes you yawn. Hey, are you yawning right now?

Fill in each sentence with the correct word:

Kingdom   Freedom   Boredom   Wisdom

1. The great _____ and experience of her grandma always amazed Rebecca.

2. You can tell that _____ has set in when you watch a person snoring in the middle of the lecture.

3. People living in a _____ ruled by a single monarch are always in danger of losing their _____.

Choose the correct definition:

1. **Wisdom**
   a. being bored
   b. the teeth in the back of the mouth
   c. having a king
   d. the state of being wise

2. **Boredom**
   a. a country with a king
   b. the state of being free
   c. the state of being bored, dullness
   d. the condition of being wise

3. **Freedom**
   a. being free, independent
   b. being wise
   c. the state of being bored
   d. a country or nation

4. **Kingdom**
   a. a country led by a king
   b. a country with democracy
   c. the state of being wise
   d. the condition of being bored

Make a sentence with each of the following words:

Wisdom   Boredom   Freedom

Challenge Words, look up these words in the dictionary:

Stardom   Random

The knight: *Sire, in your honor I bravely fought your enemies in North and South of your* **kingdom**.
King: *But I never had any enemies in the South.*
The knight: *Now you do, my lord!*

Big Words for Little Kids

DIC and DICT

The Latin roots **dic** and **dict** mean **say** or **declare**.

Dictate: to command, order; announce, say or read aloud,
On the first day of school, my teacher <u>dictated</u> the class rules.
On the first day of school, my teacher <u>announced</u> the class rules.

Dictionary: a book that lists words and their meaning
Carl didn't know what the word meant, so he looked it up in a <u>dictionary</u>.
Carl didn't know what the word meant, so he looked it up in the <u>book that lists words and their meaning</u>.

Predict: to guess what will happen in the future
Scientists <u>predict</u> that the giant panda might go extinct.
Scientists <u>guess that in the future</u> the giant panda might go extinct.

Indicate: to point out; to say briefly or suggest
I politely <u>indicated</u> to him that we could not take him but he didn't understand.
I politely <u>suggested</u> to him that we could not take him but he didn't understand.

Contradict: to speak out against something, to disagree, to argue
When Kelly said that vanilla is the best ice cream, I <u>contradicted</u> her.
When Kelly said that vanilla is the best ice cream, I <u>disagreed</u> with her.

Tidbit

Thomas Edison invented the first sound recording device in 1877. He never thought that people would be interested in recorded music but thought it might be useful for recording speech. Soon, the **Dictaphone** became a popular tool used for recording speeches. The first **Dictaphone** was made of wax cylinders and needles. In 1939 the electronic recorder was invented. Today, a modern **dictaphone,** also called a tape recorder,can fit in your pocket and record several hours of speech and music.

Fill in each sentence with the correct word:

Dictionary   Contradict   Dictate   Predict   Indicate

1. I _____ that it's going to rain today so don't you dare _____ me.

2. Bryan was having trouble spelling the word "dictate," so he looked it up in a _____.

3. My little sister loves to argue and always _____ everyone in the family.

4. The referee pointed to his watch to _____ that the game was over.

5. Please _____ the new words to me and I will try to spell them.

Choose the correct definition:

1. **Dictate**
   a. a book of words
   b. to write a letter
   c. to command
   d. to speak up against

2. **Predict**
   a. to point out
   b. to record sound
   c. to say something out loud
   d. to guess about the future

3. **Indicate**
   a. to disagree
   b. to guess about the future
   c. to point out
   d. to correct something

4. **Contradict**
   a. to disagree
   b. to guess about the future
   c. to point out
   d. to correct something

Make a sentence with each of the following words:

Dictate   Predict   Contradict   Indicate

Challenge Words, look up these words in the dictionary:

Indicator   Malediction (remember, mal means bad)

The son of a weather reporter asks his dad:
*Can you always **predict** the rain?*
***Dad:** Of course, but sometimes the dates don't match.*

TRANS

The prefix **trans-** means **across**.

Transport: to carry or move from place to place
Sally <u>transported</u> her science project from her house to school.
Sally <u>carried</u> her science project from her house to school.

Translate: to change from one form to another, from language to another
Lim <u>translated</u> his essay from English to French.
Lim <u>changed the language of</u> his essay from English to French.

Transmitter: a device that sends signal across
Radio <u>transmitters</u> are usually put on towers or mountains so they reach everyone in the city.
Radio <u>devices that send signals</u> are usually put on towers or mountains so they reach everyone in the city.

Transform: to change the form or appearance
At midnight the coach <u>transformed</u> back into a pumpkin.
At midnight the coach <u>changed its appearance</u> back into a pumpkin.

Transpire: to come about, happen, or occur, to become obvious
Robert told us how the events of his surprise party had <u>transpired</u>.
Robert told us a how the events of his surprise party had <u>happened</u>.

Tidbit

Charles Lindbergh was the first person to make a solo, nonstop, **transatlantic** flight on a plane. On May 21, 1927, this heroic American pilot stunned the world by landing in Paris after flying from New York. Lindbergh's amazing trip across the Atlantic Ocean in *The Spirit of St. Louis* took over 33 hours. It is said that Lindbergh did not sleep for a period of over 55 hours. Upon his return to the United States, he received a hero's welcome, was promoted to Colonel, and toured the country to promote interest in flight.

Fill in each sentence with the correct word:

Transport   Translator   Transmitters   Transformed

1. The doctor asked for the help of a _____ to talk to the man from Korea.

2. It was painful to see how time _____ his beautiful face.

3. Mom made sure the van was big enough to _____ all of us and the entire luggage from our house to the airport.

4. The satellites are radio _____ in the sky that let everyone get the signals everywhere on the earth.

Choose the correct definition:

1. **Transport**
   a. to move things
   b. to travel across the Atlantic
   c. to stand still
   d. to travel empty handed

2. **Translate**
   a. to order a cup of coffee
   b. to change appearance
   c. change from one language to another
   d. to travel to a foreign country

3. **Transmitter**
   a. to travel across the Atlantic
   b. carrying mittens
   c. a tower that sends signals
   d. change from one language to another

4. **Transform**
   a. to travel abroad
   b. a children toy
   c. to change appearance
   d. to happen in the past

Make a sentence with each of the following words:

Transpire   Translate   Transport

Challenge Words, look up these words in the dictionary:

Transaction   Transcontinental

An old gentleman comes over to a group of teenagers playing in a band, screaming the songs at the top of their lungs:
Gentleman: *It's a real shame they don't **transmit** your songs on the radio.*
Teenagers: *Do you like our songs?*
Gentleman: *Not really, but if you were on the radio, I could turn you off.*

MEM

The root **mem** means **memory**.

Memory: the ability to recall or remember information
Cindy never forgets anything - she has a great <u>memory</u>.
Cindy never forgets anything - she can <u>recall information</u> very well.

Memento: a reminder of the past, a souvenir
On the desk Cathy kept a <u>memento</u> of her trip to Paris.
On the desk Cathy kept a <u>reminder, a souvenir</u> of her trip to Paris.

Memorial: monument or festival in respect of the memory of a person or an event.
Don't miss Lincoln <u>Memorial</u> when you visit Washington, D.C.
Don't miss Lincoln <u>Monument</u> when you visit Washington, D.C.

Memo: a short note or reminder, short for *memorandum*
The principal sent out a <u>memo</u> telling everyone that the copy machine was broken.
The principal sent out a <u>note</u> telling everyone that the copy machine was broken.

Memoir: a story of a personal experience or past memory
Many people write <u>memoirs</u> when they get older.
Many people write <u>story of their lives</u> when they get older.

Tidbit

 Memorial Day is an American holiday observed in late May. Previously called Decoration Day, this holiday began in 1868 with the purpose of decorating the graves of Civil War veterans. Over the years, **Memorial Day** has become a day on which all soldiers who have fought and died in U.S. wars are **remembered** and honored. In Washington D.C. a wreath is placed on the Tomb of the Unknown Soldier in Arlington National Cemetery. People also put flags and flowers on the veterans' graves.

Fill in each sentence with the correct word:

Memories   Remembered   Memo   Memoir

1. Mr. Grant sent a _____ telling everyone that he was going to Hawaii for a month.

2. They say that an elephant never forgets, which means these big animals have excellent _____.

3. I learned a lot about our former president when I read his _____.

4. Sharon suddenly _____ that she forgot to feed her dog before leaving.

Choose the correct definition:

1. **Memory**
   a. a person who writes memos
   b. the ability to recall
   c. the ability to forget
   d. the written account of a person's life

2. **Memo**
   a. a personal story
   b. a short note or reminder
   c. a kind of elephant
   d. a souvenir

3. **Memoir**
   a. a short note or reminder
   b. the ability to recall
   c. a personal story
   d. an reminder

4. **Memento**
   a. bring to mind again
   b. a short notice
   c. a reminder
   d. a brief interval of time

Make a sentence with each of the following words:

Memento   Memo   Memory

Challenge Words, look up these words in the dictionary:

Commemorate   Memorabilia   Memorial

> **Nurse**: Do you **remember** your birthday?
> **Ashley**: October 6.
> **Nurse**: What year?
> **Ashley**: Every year!

VAC

The Latin root **vac** means **empty**.

Vacant: empty, not occupied
Emily's dad chose the <u>vacant</u> parking lot for her first driving lesson.
Emily's dad chose the <u>empty</u> parking lot for her first driving lesson.

Vacation: a rest from work, a break, a holiday
Julie was really excited about going on <u>vacation</u> to Hawaii.
Julie was really excited about going on <u>a holiday</u> to Hawaii.

Evacuate: to leave, make empty
During the fire drills at school, we had to <u>evacuate</u> the building and stay outside.
During the fire drills at school, we had to <u>leave</u> the building and stay outside.

Vacuous: empty of thought, empty-headed, stupid
Watching Ted's <u>vacuous</u> look, Lacy knew he was spacing out and not paying attention.
Watching Ted's <u>empty-headed</u> look, Lacy knew he was spacing out and not paying attention.

Tidbit

The word **vacuum** has two meanings. One type of **vacuum** refers to outer space, which is so empty that air doesn't even exist. The other refers to a machine that sucks dust and dirt out of your carpet. In 1901, the British engineer H. Cecil Booth invented one of the first **vacuum** cleaners, known as Puffing Billy. It was a huge, horse-drawn, gasoline powered machine that was parked outside the house that needed cleaning and had long hoses that were fed through the windows. A whole group of cleaners had to move the vacuum from house to house. I bet **vacuuming** *your* house doesn't sound so hard anymore! Nowadays, we have robot vacuums that will work while you are not even home.

Fill in each sentence with the correct word:

Vacuous   Evacuate   Vacation   Vacant

1. The Johnson's house is _____ now that they are gone on a long _____ in Hawaii for a year.

2. Terry wasn't scared when they had to _____ the plane; going down the inflatable slide was a fun way to start her _____.

3. The teacher tried to explain the physics laws, but after looking at a sea of _____ faces, she gave up.

Choose the correct definition:

1. **Vacant**
   a. stupid, empty-headed
   b. a rest from work
   c. to leave
   d. empty, not occupied

2. **Evacuate**
   a. a kind of fun
   b. to leave, make empty
   c. a vacuum
   d. a rest from work

3. **Vacation**
   a. a rest from work, a break
   b. empty
   c. to leave, make empty
   d. a profession

4. **Vacuous**
   a. not occupied
   b. empty-headed, blank, stupid
   c. a machine
   d. some shows on the television

Make a sentence with each of the following words:

Vacant   Evacuate   Vacation   Vacuous

Challenge Words, look up these words in the dictionary:

Vacate   Vacancy

Teacher: *Erik, how do you imagine a perfect school?*
Erik: *Vacant.*

VIS and VID

The Latin roots **vis** and **vid** mean **to see**.

Vision: eyesight OR a mental picture; idea
Because of poor <u>vision</u>, Charlie had to wear glasses every day.
Because of poor <u>eyesight</u>, Charlie had to wear glasses every day.

Looking at his back yard, Tom had a <u>vision</u> of blooming fruit trees.
Looking at his back yard, Tom had a <u>mental picture</u> of blooming fruit trees.

Visualize: to form a mental picture, to imagine
When Joey decided to build a robot, he <u>visualized</u> it with a flamethrower and huge crab-like arms.
When Joey decided to build a robot, he <u>imagined</u> it with a flamethrower and huge crab-like arms.

Evident: clearly seen, obvious
When Joanna was afraid to turn the page: it was <u>evident</u> that the book was scary.
When Joanna was afraid to turn the page: it was <u>obvious</u> that the book was scary.

Provision (prefix pro means ahead of time): supply of food, a preparation ahead of time
The expedition was nearly out of <u>provisions</u> by the end of the journey.
The expedition was nearly out of it's <u>supply of food</u> by the end of the journey.

Tidbit

 We've all seen *camouflage*, the clothes that soldiers wear to blend in with things around them and become **invisible**. For the jungle, army fatigues are green and olive; for the desert, they're tan and brown. But now, the military is in the process of making clothes that have little cameras in them that look at a soldier's surroundings and project the image onto the cloth. A soldier standing in front of a brick wall would actually look like the wall and a soldier standing in front of a tree will blend in with the tree. He'll be practically **invisible**!

Fill in each sentence with the correct word:

Visualize   Evident   Invisible   Provision   Vision

1. Evan tried to shrink into the corner and cover his face with a book so he would be _____ when the teacher began asking questions.

2. The contract had a special_____ for late payment.

3. Getting ready to go to the ice cream store, Jordan could _____ how good everything was going to look and taste.

4. Tyler had a _____ of himself as a race car driver every time he got into his dad's Mustang.

5. It was _____ that Erica was trying to be the teacher's pet by the way she always raised her hand in class.

Choose the correct definition:

1. **Vision**
   a. unmistakable
   b. eyesight or an idea
   c. unseen
   d. bad dreams

2. **Visualize**
   a. eyesight
   b. hidden
   c. to imagine
   d. obvious

3. **Evident**
   a. to imagine
   b. idea
   c. eyesight
   d. clearly seen, obvious

4. **Invisible**
   a. not able to be seen, hidden
   b. eyesight
   c. obvious
   d. visible

Make a sentence with each of the following words:

Vision   Visualize   Evident   Provision

Challenge Words, look up these words in the dictionary:

Evidence   Provide   Visionary

> **Teacher**: *Johnny, I hope this time I won't find any **evidence** of your cheating on the test.*
> **Johnny**: *I hope so too, sir.*

AMPHI and AMBI

The Greek prefixes **amphi-** and **ambi-** mean **two, both,** or **on both sides**.

Amphibious: able to live or operate on both land and water
You often find frogs near ponds and rivers because they are <u>amphibious</u> animals.
You often find frogs near ponds and rivers because they are <u>able to live on both land and water</u>.

Ambidextrous: able to use both hands with equal skill
Jackie can switch hands in the middle of her writing because she is <u>ambidextrous</u>.
Jackie can switch hands in the middle of her writing because she <u>uses both hands equally well</u>.

Ambiguous: having two meanings; vague, unclear
Derek was being <u>ambiguous</u> when he talked about "those guys" who took his skateboard.
Derek was being <u>unclear</u> when he talked about "those guys" who took his skateboard.

Ambivalent: having a mixture of opposite feelings
Joyce felt <u>ambivalent</u> about going to the camp because she knew it would be fun but she'd miss her friends.
Joyce had <u>mixed and opposite feelings</u> about going to the camp because she knew it would be fun but she'd miss her friends.

Tidbit

 Have you ever heard of a Duck Tour? These tours allow you to drive across town, over hills, and then right into a lake or river without sinking, because you take your tour in an **amphibious** vehicle. The first such vehicle had a steam engine and was called *Orukter Amphibolous*. It was designed and built by an American inventor Oliver Evans in 1805, though there is no record that it actually moved by itself over land or water. These "cars" were also used in World War II to carry supplies from boats to land. Today's Duck Tour **amphibious** vehicles have modern design and machinery and are used for fun tours in many cities such as Boston and San Francisco.

Fill in each sentence with the correct word:

Amphibious   Ambivalent   Ambidextrous   Ambiguous

1. Joseph noticed that Megan was _____ when he saw her drawing a picture with one hand while writing something down with the other.

2. Some cars are made to be _____ and can be driven right into the water.

3. The coach's instructions were so_____ that no one on the team knew what position to play.

4. Greg felt _____ about taking the school bus because he could go to school with his friends, but he'd have to wake up early.

Choose the correct definition:

1. **Amphibious**
   a. using both hands
   b. able to live on land and water
   c. a lizard
   d. a mixture of opposite feelings

2. **Ambidextrous**
   a. able to use both hands well
   b. a mixture of opposite feelings
   c. having two meanings
   d. able to live on land and water

3. **Ambiguous**
   a. something big
   b. a mixture of opposite feelings
   c. vague, unclear
   d. able to live on land

4. **Ambivalent**
   a. a mixture of opposite feelings
   b. carries sick people
   c. able to live on land
   d. good with both hands

Make a sentence with each of the following words:

Amphibious   Ambidextrous   Ambiguous   Ambivalent

Challenge Words, look up these words in the dictionary:

Amphora

> The teacher calls on Seymour, the captain's son.
> **Teacher**: Who can live equally well on both land and water?
> **Seymour**: The sailors.

MIS

The prefix **mis** means **wrong**, **bad**, or **hate**.

Mistake: an error or fault
Jake did excellent on his math homework, making only one mistake in thirty problems.
Jake did excellent on his math homework, making only one error in thirty problems.

Misgivings: doubts, worries, second thoughts
Jerry had big misgivings about walking down the dark path alone.
Jerry had big worries about walking down the dark path alone.

Misbehavior: bad behavior, acting up
When Al slammed the door in anger, he was punished for his misbehavior.
When Al slammed the door in anger, he was punished for his bad behavior.

Mistrust: not having trust, have doubts about
Tricked by Kim in the past, Dave learned to mistrust her friendly smile.
Tricked by Kim in the past, Dave learned to have doubts about her friendly smile.

Miscalculate: to make a mistake, either in counting or thinking
The pilot miscalculated and landed five miles east of the airport.
The pilot made a mistake in counting and landed five miles east of the airport.

Tidbit

Miscalculations can be very costly. The Hubble Space Telescope, completed in 1990 at a cost of $1.5 billion, was expected to provide the best and clearest view of the universe. Made with very powerful cameras and mirrors, the Hubble Telescope was launched to its orbit from the space shuttle *Discovery*. Soon after, however, tests showed that the shape of the Hubble Space Telescope's mirrors was **miscalculated**. The images sent to the Earth from the telescope were blurry. Astronauts repaired the telescope in 1993 by adding and replacing critical parts while the telescope was still in orbit.

Fill in each sentence with the correct word:

Mistake   Misgivings   Misbehavior   Miscalculation

1. A slight _____ early in his arithmetic caused the scientist to make a much bigger _____ in his conclusion.

2. Though Sharon had _____ about disciplining her son too harshly, sometimes it seemed necessary due to his constant _____.

3. Michael was caught stealing, so now he is having _____ about his_____ .

4. The Mars researchers made a _____ in their numbers which made the Mars Explorer crash land on the planet.

Choose the correct definition:

1. **Mistake**
   a. an error or fault
   b. perfect
   c. improper conduct
   d. doubt about the result of an action

2. **Misgivings**
   a. an error or fault
   b. never giving to charity
   c. doubt about the result of an action
   d. a neighbor

3. **Misbehavior**
   a. doubt about the result of an action
   b. improper conduct
   c. an error in counting or thinking
   d. being on your best behavior

4. **Mistrust**
   a. not having trust
   b. an error in counting
   c. perfect mate
   d. friendly smile

Make a sentence with each of the following words:

Mistake   Misbehavior   Misgivings   Mistrust

Challenge Words, look up these words in the dictionary:

Misanthrope   Mischievous   Misguided   Misadventure

Teacher: *There's not a single **mistake** in your homework, Bill. Was anyone helping your father?*

LAV, LAU, and LUT

The Latin roots **lav-**, **lau-**, and **lut-** mean **to wash**.

Laundry: clothes that need washing; a place where clothes are washed
William had so much dirty <u>laundry</u> in his room you couldn't see the carpet.
William had so many <u>clothes that needed washing</u> in his room you couldn't see the carpet.

Dilute: to add water, water down
Ronald had to <u>dilute</u> the mouthwash so that it wouldn't burn his mouth.
Ronald had to <u>water down</u> the mouthwash so that it wouldn't burn his mouth.

Lavatory: a bathroom, a place where you can wash up
Mark thought about not washing his hands because the <u>lavatory</u> line was so long.
Mark thought about not washing his hands because the <u>bathroom</u> line was so long.

Lavish: plentiful, generous, spending money like water
Sarah's rich aunt showered her with <u>lavish</u> gifts every time she came to visit.
Sarah's rich aunt showered her with <u>generous and luxurious</u> gifts every time she came to visit.

Tidbit

 Lavender is a flower in the mint family. The name probably comes from the Latin verb *lavare*: to wash. Ancient Greek and Romans used lavender in their bathwater. A military doctor at that time wrote that **lavender** was able to treat headaches, sore throats, and even burns! Romans **lavishly** applied **lavender** oils to their hair, cloths, beds, and even to their walls. Later, 16th century French glove makers would scent their gloves with **lavender**, claiming that it would keep sickness away. There is probably some truth to this as fleas, who are known to carry disease, don't like **lavender**.

Fill in each sentence with the correct word:

Laundry　　　　　　Dilute　　　　　　Lavatory　　　　　Lavish

1. In the middle of a family trip, Tina suddenly needed to use the _____ after drinking a large soda.

2. The first time Andrew did his _____, he used too much soap and foam started coming out of the washing machine!

3. The surgeon put a _____ amount of soap on his hands and thoroughly washed them.

4. Charlie knew from chemistry that if you wanted to _____ acid, you had to pour acid into the water as doing otherwise may cause acid to splash on your skin.

Choose the correct definition:

1. **Laundry**
   a. a bathroom
   b. the stuff you should never do
   c. to make something weaker
   d. dirty clothes

2. **Dilute**
   a. to water down
   b. plentiful
   c. dirty clothes
   d. a Laundromat

3. **Lavatory**
   a. a bathroom
   b. hot lava
   c. luxurious
   d. dirty clothes

4. **Lavish**
   a. to make a liquid watery
   b. generous, luxurious
   c. dirty clothes
   d. a bathroom

Make a sentence with each of the following words:

Laundry　　　　　　Dilute　　　　　　Lavatory　　　　　Lavish

Challenge Words, look up these words in the dictionary:

Ablution　　　　　　Pollution

A little boy watching a cow drinking from a pond asks:
*Why does the cow **dilute** her milk with water?*

JUS and JUD

The Latin root **jus** means **law**, while **jud** means **judge** or **lawyer.**

Judgment: a ruling, decision, or conclusion
Rachel's <u>judgment</u> was that Shrek was the best cartoon character of all time.
Rachel's <u>conclusion</u> was that Shrek was the best cartoon character of all time.

Justice: fairness, supported by the laws; fair treatment
Darren accepted that there was <u>justice</u> in his parent's decision to ground him after he lied about not doing his homework.
Darren accepted that there was <u>fairness</u> in his parent's decision to ground him after he lied about not doing his homework.

Prejudice: a preset idea, deciding before knowing the facts, usually negative
Nick was <u>prejudiced</u> against eggplant because he hated purple things.
Nick thought he <u>wouldn't like</u> eggplant <u>even before trying</u> because he hated purple things.

Judicious: reasonable, well thought-out, careful, sensible
Ronald applied a <u>judicious</u> amount of sunscreen over his entire body.
Ronald applied a <u>reasonable</u> amount of sunscreen over his entire body.

Tidbit

 Justice is the fair and equal treatment of all people under the laws. One of the oldest sets of laws in history is the Code of Hammurabi. Altogether, 282 laws and the punishments were engraved on a huge pillar and given to King Hammurabi in ancient Mesopotamia almost 4,000 years ago. Some of the laws seem pretty harsh in modern times. One of them says that if a son hits his father, the son's hands should be cut off. Some other laws forced death sentences for stealing property or children. Yet another stated that "If a man knocks out the teeth of his equal, his teeth shall be knocked out."

Fill in each sentence with the correct word:

Judicious   Prejudice   Justice   Judgment

1. Chris thought that _____ was done when the school bully got suspended.

2. Dan thought it was a _____ decision to wear a cape to school dance, but his brother burst out laughing and said he looked silly.

3. Camellia never really understood _____. How could someone judge other people without ever meeting them?

4. When twins were arguing about something, they always went to their mom who made the _____ about who did what and who was to blame.

Choose the correct definition:

1. **Judgment**
   a. a judge
   b. fairness
   c. a jury
   d. a ruling, decision, or conclusion

2. **Justice**
   a. sensible, careful
   b. fairness under the law
   c. a decision
   d. a name

3. **Prejudice**
   a. a preset negative idea
   b. careful, sensible
   c. not liking broccoli
   d. unfairness

4. **Judicious**
   a. fairness
   b. reasonable, well thought-out
   c. a ruling or conclusion
   d. a delicious juice

Make a sentence with each of the following words:

Judicious   Prejudice   Judgment   Justice

Challenge Words, look up these words in the dictionary:

Justify   Injustice

*If your neighbors played loud music until 2 A.M., would it be **judicious** to call them at 4 A.M. to tell them how much you enjoyed it?*

PHIL

The Greek root **phil** means **love**.

Philanthropy: charity, generosity; giving out of love for humankind
Mrs. Lopez was so devoted to <u>philanthropy</u> that she gave away everything she had.
Mrs. Lopez was so devoted to <u>charity and generosity</u> that she gave away everything she had.

Philanthropist: a generous person, one who gives money to a person or cause
Reuben was a <u>philanthropist</u> who gave his entire fortune to save the forests.
Reuben was a <u>generous person</u> who gave his entire fortune to save the forests.

Philosophy: study of knowledge and reason; one's opinion of "the meaning of life"
Philosopher: a person who studies philosophy
<u>Philosophers</u> try to understand the meaning of life, but Kayla's <u>philosophy</u> is "to just have fun."
<u>People who study philosophy</u> try to understand the meaning of life, but Kayla's <u>opinion of "the meaning of life"</u> is "to just have fun."

Bibliophile: someone who loves books, a book lover
Kyle, a <u>bibliophile</u>, got in trouble for reading a mystery novel in the middle of his math class!
Kyle, a <u>book lover</u>, got in trouble for reading a mystery novel in the middle of his math class!

Tidbit

The term *philia* at the end of a word indicates a love of something. The ending *phile* at the end of a word is for a person who loves. The root at the beginning of the word tells you what is loved. There are many "philes" in the world. A **Francophile** is a person who loves French, while a **Turophile** is someone who loves cheese. An **Arctophile** is someone who loves and collects teddy bears. Take a look at some of these other "loves":

Ailurophilia: Love of cats
Halophilia: Love of salt or salt-water
Philalethia: Love of the truth
Xylophilia: Love of wood

Chrysophilia: Love of gold
Heliophilia: Love of sunlight
Stegophilia: Love of climbing buildings
Thalassophilia: Love of the ocean

Fill in each sentence with the correct word:

Philanthropist   Bibliophile   Philanthropy   Philosophy

1. They called Kevin a _____ because he always carried a book with him and read whenever he could.

2. His _____ was that the only way to avoid getting bored is always having a book with you.

3. Although Katie didn't consider herself a true _____, she always shared her lunch with others.

4. At first, Scrooge believed _____ was a waste of money.

Choose the correct definition:

1. **Philanthropy**
   a. someone who loves books
   b. someone who shares
   c. charity and generosity
   d. the love of wisdom

2. **Philosophy**
   a. study of knowledge
   b. the love of people
   c. the love of people named Phil
   d. charity and generosity

3. **Bibliophile**
   a. a person that loves books
   b. one who loves cats
   c. someone who loves people
   d. the love of wisdom

4. **Philanthropist**
   a. a book reader
   b. a generous person
   c. one who loves wisdom
   d. someone who loves cats

Make a sentence with each of the following words:

Philanthropy   Philosophy   Arctophile (one who loves teddy bears)

Challenge Words, look up these words in the dictionary:

Philharmonic (hint: harmonic means music)
Philately

History Teacher: *Ted, what can you tell us about famous* **philosophers** *of ancient Greece?*
Ted: *They are all dead.*

SOME

This suffix means **describing a thing, quality** or **action**.

Gruesome: causing horror and disgust, shocking and scary
Sean couldn't watch the <u>gruesome</u> movie and hid behind his popcorn.
Sean couldn't watch the <u>scary</u> movie and hid behind his popcorn.

Awesome: anything that fills one with awe (wonder and fear), whether beautiful, powerful, or terrible
Everyone just stood and stared as the <u>awesome</u> tornado rolled into town.
Everyone just stood and stared as the <u>powerful</u> tornado rolled into town.

Meddlesome: someone who is nosy, interfering, intrusive
Our <u>meddlesome</u> neighbor was always telling us what's wrong with our lawn.
Our <u>nosy and intrusive</u> neighbor was always telling us what's wrong with our lawn.

Handsome: good-looking
After Tommy grew 6 inches and got a decent haircut, the girls started saying he was <u>handsome</u>.
After Tommy grew 6 inches and got a decent haircut, the girls started saying he <u>looked good.</u>

Tidbit

Just like you shouldn't judge a book by its cover, neither should you trust a word's appearance to tell you the whole story. The word **handsome**, for example, used to mean *handy*. After all, **handsome** is just the word *hand* with the suffix *some*. Using your hands has other meanings too, and until the late 1500's, **handsome** also meant easy to control. Another interesting word is **gruesome**. The *grue* in **gruesome** comes from a word meaning *grow*, but *gruesome* has nothing to do with a growing horror or disgust. In fact, **gruesome's** meaning comes from a "to shiver or shudder with fear or cold."

Fill in each sentence with the correct word:

Handsome   Meddlesome   Awesome   Gruesome

1. Whenever she was in the wood shop, Elise became nervous by imagining _____ pictures of people getting their fingers cut off.

2. The fireworks that lit up the sky were _____.

3. It was such a _____ horse that Brad thought riding it would be exciting fun.

4. The _____ reporters found out about the crooked politician's schemes.

Choose the correct definition:

1. **Gruesome**
   a. a pumpkin
   b. inspiring awe
   c. causing horror, disgust, and fear
   d. liking to interfere

2. **Awesome**
   a. something that fills you with awe
   b. the cool new video game
   c. disgusting and scary
   d. attractive and sweet

3. **Meddlesome**
   a. old neighbors
   b. someone who is nosy
   c. new neighbors
   d. a German composer

4. **Handsome**
   a. a movie star
   b. inspiring awe
   c. disgusting
   d. good-looking

Make a sentence with each of the following words:

Gruesome   Awesome   Meddlesome   Handsome

Challenge Words, look up these words in the dictionary:

Fearsome   Winsome

Q: *Is it true that you a have a very* **handsome** *brother?*
A: *No, but my brother has one.*

CULE, ICLE and LING

These suffixes mean **very small**.

Minuscule: very small, tiny
An ant is <u>minuscule</u> when compared to a dog.
An ant is <u>tiny</u> when compared to a dog.

Article: a short piece of writing or story; small words, like *the, an* and *a*
James wrote an interesting <u>article</u> about the new math teacher.
James wrote an interesting <u>short story</u> about the new math teacher.

Particle: a very small piece or part
He screamed with pain when a dust <u>particle</u> got in his eye.
He screamed with pain when a <u>small piece</u> of dust got in his eye.

Sapling: a small, young tree
The <u>sapling</u> we planted five years ago has turned into a tall tree.
The <u>small tree</u> we planted five years ago has turned into a tall tree.

Sibling: brother or sister
Then he told me he had nine <u>siblings</u>.
Then he told me he had nine <u>brothers and sisters</u>.

Tidbit

The word **molecule** which means a "very tiny particle" in French, was brought in by French philosopher René Descartes. **Molecules** are made of two or more atoms held together by chemical bonds. The smallest **molecule** is hydrogen gas, made of two hydrogen atoms joined together. The word hydrogen comes from the roots hydro, meaning water and gen, meaning born, because when burned it made water. In contrast, **macromolecules** (macro means large) are made of thousands and even millions of **particles**.

Fill in each sentence with the correct word:

Sibling　　　　　Minuscule　　　　　Article　　　　　Sapling

1. Johnny worried that the newspaper _____ he wrote about his favorite team was too long.

2. The difference in size between a _____ and a large bush is huge.

3. James never talked about his family, so I didn't know if he had a _____.

4. When he peered through the glass, he could see hundreds of _____ bugs.

Choose the correct definition:

1. **Minuscule**
   a. a small purse
   b. very small
   c. a type of mouse
   d. a small piece of writing

2. **Article**
   a. a piece of clothing
   b. very small
   c. a small piece of writing
   d. to belittle or insult

3. **Sapling**
   a. a small tree
   b. a small part
   c. a short piece of writing
   d. a brother or sister

4. **Sibling**
   a. a small piece of writing
   b. a brother or sister
   c. a small tree
   d. a small handbag

Make a sentence with each of the following words:

Minuscule　　　　　Article　　　　　Ridicule　　　　　Particle

Challenge Words, look up these words in the dictionary:

Cuticle (hint: cutis means skin)　　　　　Duckling
Icicle (not really a challenging word)

Q: *Who are you?*
A: *I am a thief!*
Q: *But why are you so **minuscule**?*
A: *I am a pocket thief.*

LEG

One of the meanings of the Latin root **leg** is **law**.

Legacy: inheritance, a gift of property left by a will, tradition
Grandpa's <u>legacy</u> to all his grandchildren was his rare coin collection.
Grandpa's <u>gift after he died</u> to all his grandchildren was his rare coin collection.

Legitimate: lawful, real, rightful
Billy should have been the <u>legitimate</u> winner since the person he played against cheated.
Billy should have been the <u>real</u> winner since the person he played against cheated.

Legal: lawful, according to the law, allowed by law
It's <u>legal</u> to sell cookies to people at their houses, but not to throw eggs at them.
It's <u>allowed by law</u> to sell cookies to people at their houses, but not to throw eggs at them.

Illegal: not legal, not allowed by law, against the law
Some cities have made motor scooters <u>illegal</u> because of the noise they make.
Some cities make it <u>against the law</u> to ride motor scooters because of the noise they make.

Tidbit

There are a lot of really weird laws out there. Here's a list of some things that are **illegal** in America (not really!):

• In Michigan, a husband **legally** owns his wife's hair.

• It's against the law to catch fish with your bare hands in Kansas.

• In Pueblo, Colorado, it's **illegal** to let a dandelion grow within city limits.

• It is **illegal** to lie down and fall asleep with your shoes on in North Dakota.

• In Nogales, Arizona, it's against the law to wear suspenders.

• In Atlanta, Georgia, it's **illegal** to tie a giraffe to a telephone pole or street lamp.

Fill in each sentence with the correct word:

Legal   Legacy   Legitimate   Illegal

1. Samantha knew it was _____ to ride her bike without a helmet.

2. Mr. Dumas told everyone that he was now the _____ owner of the house.

3. Every generation leaves a _____ to the next generation by which it is remembered.

4. Jason made the best of his _____ right to speak out against the salary cuts.

Choose the correct definition:

1. **Legal**
   a. by the law
   b. invalid

   c. inheritance
   d. a protected bird

2. **Legacy**
   a. a collection
   b. not fair

   c. an inheritance or tradition
   d. genuine

3. **Legitimate**
   a. long legged
   b. real, lawful

   c. inheritance
   d. a president

4. **Illegal**
   a. lawful
   b. awful

   c. against the law
   d. horrible

Make a sentence with each of the following words:

Legal   Legacy   Legitimate

Challenge Words, look up these words in the dictionary:

Legislature   Legalized   Paralegal

A policeman stops a car and recognizes the driver as his old English teacher. "How are you Mrs. Brown? Now get out a piece of paper and a pen and write 100 times "I will not be making illegal left turns.""

MAN and MANU

These roots mean **by hand**.

Manicure: the care of hands and nails
Once a month, Mia drives into town for a manicure.
Once a month, Mia drives into town to get her hands and nails done.

Manufacture: to make something by hand or with machinery
The workers manufacture small plastic toys for children.
The workers make small plastic toys for children by hand.

Manually: by hand
In the ancient times, all work was done manually.
In the ancient times, all work was done by hand.

Manipulate: to work out or manage; to influence someone by lying, to trick
Bobby manipulated his mom so she'd let him stay home from school by pretending to have a stomach ache.
Bobby tricked his mom so she'd let him stay home from school by pretending to have a stomach ache.

Manuscript: any handwritten text; a proposed book sent to a publisher
Mark Twain brought a manuscript of *The Adventures of Tom Sawyer* to a publisher.
Mark Twain brought his handwritten book of *The Adventures of Tom Sawyer* to a publisher.

Tidbit

The word **manuscript** means "written by hand" in Latin.. In ancient Egypt, scribes, people hired to write books or documents by hand, used paper-like material made from papyrus plant. In Russia, the birch bark was used for the **manuscripts**. In Europe they used parchment, a thin material made from calfskin, sheepskin or goatskin. China was the country where paper as we know it was first invented during the second century. The **manufacturing** of paper started in Europe about 700 years ago and quickly spread over the continent.

Fill in each sentence with the correct word:

Manually   Manicure   Manuscript   Manufacture

1. Many companies _____ bicycles and motorcycles.

2. Farming is hard work and most of it is still done_____ .

3. Getting a _____ is important if you want to keep your hands and nails looking beautiful and clean.

4. Most authors write a _____ before sending the book to the printer.

Choose the correct definition:

1. **Manicure**
   a. to care for one's hands
   b. to make by hand
   c. to heal with hands
   d. to work out by hand

2. **Manual**
   a. by hand
   b. to care for one's hands
   c. to invent something
   d. handcuffs

3. **Manufacture**
   a. to work out
   b. to make by hand
   c. a store
   d. to see something new

4. **Manuscript**
   a. nice handwriting
   b. a handwritten book
   c. to care for one's hands
   d. an author

Make a sentence with each of the following words:

Manicure   Manufacture   Manual   Manipulate

Challenge Words, look up these words in the dictionary:

Maneuver   Manifest   Manipulate

*Little Oswald brought from the library the book, "**Manual** to Raise a Healthy Child."*
Mom: *What are you going to do with this book?*
Oswald: *I want to find out if you are taking good care of me.*

FIN and FINIS

The Latin roots **fin** and **finis** mean **end** or **limit**.

Finish: to complete or reach the end
Kevin had to <u>finish</u> his book report before Tuesday.
Kevin had to <u>complete</u> his book report before Tuesday.

Confine: to keep within limits; to keep in prison
The doctor insisted that the patient stay <u>confined</u> to bed for one week.
The doctor insisted that the patient stay <u>within the limits</u> of bed for one week.

Infinite: endless, without limit
There is an <u>infinite</u> number of stars in the universe.
There is a <u>endless</u> number of stars in the universe.

Finale: an ending, usually of a show, concert, or play
We waited until the <u>finale</u> to give a standing ovation to the choir.
We waited until the <u>end of the concert</u> to give a standing ovation to the choir.

Affinity: likeness; close relationship; attraction
I have had an <u>affinity</u> for horses since my first trip to a farm as a child.
I have had an <u>attraction</u> for horses since my first trip to a farm as a child.

Tidbit

Solitary **confinement** means putting a criminal in a jail cell alone. It is used to punish very violent prisoners who might harm others. Sometimes solitary **confinement** is used to protect a prisoner from others. In the United States, solitary **confinement** was introduced in a Philadelphia prison in 1829. The most famous prison in the United States, Alcatraz, opened in 1934 and housed the worst criminals in the country. One cell, called The Hole, was a small room with bare concrete walls where Robert Stroud, known as the "Birdman of Alcatraz," lived for six years alone. Stroud got his nickname because he raised canaries in prison. Today, there are at least 25,000 U.S. prisoners in solitary **confinement**.

Fill in each sentence with the correct word:

Finale   Confine   Finish   Infinite   Affinity

1. The universe is an _____ place.

2. Humans feel an _____ to small, fluffy pets.

3. During the show, lion tamers must _____ the animals to the cages.

4. We waited for the singer to _____ her song before the band's grand _____.

Choose the correct definition:

1. **Finish**
   a. the last part of an opera
   b, a type of book report
   c. an attraction
   d. to complete something

2. **Confine**
   a. to complete
   b. to keep within limits
   c. everything is alright
   d. a prison

3. **Infinite**
   a. a small child
   b. an attraction to something
   c. without end
   d. likable

4. **Affinity**
   a. an attraction
   b. limitless or without end
   c. a very big number
   d. Greek capital

5. **Finale**
   a. to complete something
   b. limitless or without end
   c. the last part of a musical act
   d. in the beginning

Make a sentence with each of the following words:

Finish   Infinite   Finale   Confine

First kid: *I can't wait for school to be over, so I can **finish** my second book.*
Second kid: *I didn't know that you were writing a book.*
First kid: *Writing? I meant reading.*

About the Authors

Michael Levin, M.D. is a developmental and educational specialist and a child psychiatrist. He practices in Northern California and teaches at UC-Berkeley Extension. Charan Langton is an electrical engineer and a mathematician. Charan and Michael are also the authors of The Reading Lesson and The Verbal Math Lesson books.

Our Products

The Reading Lesson Book

This book has 20 step-by-step lessons for parents who want to teach their young child to read. It combines phonics and key word recognition and will take your child from no reading skills to second-grade reading level. Suitable for children as young as three years old.

The Reading Lesson CD-ROM

The CD-ROM makes reading come alive. Giggle Bunny, our little mascot, will delight your child while teaching the art of blending sounds and reading new words. This is an extensive CD-ROM with hundreds of games and activities. The CD-ROM closely follows the book but offers an entertaining and fun way to learn.

The StoryBook CD-ROM

While The Reading Lesson CD-ROM concentrates on learning new sounds and words, the StoryBook CD-ROM helps your child with real reading. The stories start simple and become longer and more complex. Sweet and attractive stories to print and make little books.

The Writing Lesson CD-ROM

Practice, practice, practice. That's what a child needs to learn to write. The Writing Lesson program brings you a collection of never-ending supply of practice worksheets. Three different styles are included in one CD - Primary, Script, and Cursive.

The Verbal Math Lesson Book Series

Verbal Math Lesson Level 1 Book - for children in K-1
Verbal Math Lesson Level 2 Book - for children in grades 1-2
More Math Lesson books to come

For more information, please see our websites
www.readinglesson.com
www.mathlesson.com